Social Work, Social Policy and Older People

Thinking Through Social Work – titles in the series

Evidence-based Practice in Social Work   ISBN 978 1 84445 611 6

Social Work, Social Policy, and Older People   ISBN 978 1 84445 349 8

To order, please contact our distributor: BEBC Distribution, Albion Close, Parkstone, Poole, BH12 3LL. Telephone: 0845 230 9000, email: learningmatters@bebc.co.uk. You can also find more information on each of these titles and our other learning resources at www.learningmatters.co.uk

Social Work, Social Policy and Older People

Edited by

ROBERT JOHNS

LearningMatters

First published in 2011 by Learning Matters Ltd

British Library Cataloguing in Publication Data
A CIP record for this book is available from the British Library

ISBN: 978 1 84445 349 8

This book is also available in the following ebook formats:

Adobe ebook ISBN: 9781844457618
EPUB ebook ISBN: 9781844457601
Kindle ISBN: 9780857250216

Cover design by Toucan Design
Text design by Topics – The Creative Partnership
Project Management by Deer Park Productions
Typeset by Pantek Arts Ltd
Printed and bound in Great Britain by Bell & Bain Ltd, Glasgow

Learning Matters Ltd
20 Cathedral Yard
Exeter EX1 1HB
Tel: 01392 215560
info@learningmatters.co.uk
www.learningmatters.co.uk

Mixed Sources
Product group from well-managed
forests and other controlled sources
www.fsc.org Cert no. TT-COC-002769
© 1996 Forest Stewardship Council

FSC

Contents

Contributors

Robert Johns

Robert Johns leads the social work education team at the University of East London, where he is principal lecturer. He has over 25 years' experience of statutory social work across the full range: youth justice, childcare, mental health, vulnerable adults and also as an independent children's guardian. With degree qualifications in social policy, law and social work, he has taught applied social work law and social policy in higher education since 1986 on both professional qualifying and post-qualifying (PQ) courses. He was a Teacher Fellow at De Montfort University and until recently led the qualifying MA in Social Work taught jointly with the Tavistock and Portman NHS Foundation Trust. At PQ level he has been involved in teaching a range of programmes, including Best Interest Assessor, Approved Mental Health Professional and Specialist Level Adult Care.

Dawn Ludick

Dawn Ludick is the Programme Leader for the qualifying MA in Social Work at the University of East London, where she is a senior lecturer. She has over 20 years' experience in statutory, voluntary sector and therapeutic work with children and their families both in South Africa and the UK, with qualifications that include a Masters in clinical social work, management qualifications, and D.Phil. in social work.

Before joining the University of East London Docklands, she worked as a manager in the voluntary sector. She teaches on various modules on the Social Work MA run in collaboration with the Tavistock and Portman NHS Foundation Trust. She is a member of the external independent evaluation team for a safeguarding initiative concerning issues of spirit possession or witchcraft funded by the City Parochial Foundation Trust for London. Her particular interests are in gestalt psychotherapy and play therapy.

Nicolette Wade

Nicolette Wade is Course Leader for the BSc Social Work programme at the Bedford campus of the University of Bedfordshire and is a principal lecturer. Since qualifying in 1983, she has worked in a number of statutory settings covering a broad range of social work responsibilities. From the mid-1990s until 2001 she was responsible for development of services for older people with both dementia and functional mental health problems in a semi-rural area of the country. This work was particularly informed by the person-centred approach developed by the late Professor Tom Kitwood. Nicolette has taught and contributed towards the development of a range of social work programmes at both undergraduate and postgraduate level, including PQ, since 1999. Specialisms include adult services, social policy and social work theory. Research interests focus on person-centred approaches and social work and spirituality.

Acknowledgements

The editor would like to acknowledge with thanks the unstinting support of Kate Lodge and Luke Block from Learning Matters in the production of this book. This book took rather longer than intended to put in its appearance, and their unswerving commitment and patience were greatly appreciated.

Also heartfelt thanks to the two major contributors to this volume: Dawn Ludick and Nicolette Wade. Dawn conducted a great deal of research and preparation for Chapter 5, familiarising herself with the unfamiliar, and setting out on a new path of producing material for publication. Nicolette offered the benefit of her years of experience in work with older people, together with her accumulated knowledge of related social work practice and social policy, most especially her deep insights into personalisation. Nicolette was responsible for much of Chapter 6 and without her this book would simply not have been possible.

Producing a long list of people to whom the author feels indebted is a temptation to be avoided, but coming to the end of a full-time career in social work education it would be remiss of me not to take the opportunity to thank all my social work education colleagues at De Montfort University and latterly at the University of East London. Your encouragement and comradeship over the years have been invaluable. I am also indebted to a significant number of social work service users from whom I have learned a great deal, and who have unwittingly offered their experiences as the basis on which the fictitious case studies in this book have been devised.

Finally, special thanks to Tina whose support has been priceless beyond measure. Forty years together and now looking forward to being 'older people' ourselves.

Robert Johns

Introduction

This book is about how social work and social policy connect

This book introduces you to the academic discipline of social policy by applying it to social work with older people. It demonstrates how social policy can help us understand the position of older people in Britain today, and also helps us to understand why social work practice takes the form that it does. This book will therefore be of interest both to social policy and social work students. It is essential for social work students to know about social policy in order to be effective practitioners: social policy provides some of the core knowledge social workers need, but equally importantly, a study of social policy enables you as a student to acquire and develop some of the essential skills you need. It will almost certainly help you demonstrate the acquisition of knowledge and attainment of skills required by Subject Benchmarks and National Occupational Standards. Academically, a study of social policy helps to develop higher-order skills with an emphasis on demonstrating understanding and application of ideas, evaluating and assessing policy changes and – naturally enough, with this being a social work book – relating all of this to a practice context. Here the practice context is work with older people, and the aim is that by applying a social policy approach, you will as a practitioner deepen your understanding of the position of older people in contemporary society and be able to reflect on, and respond to, different kinds of needs which you will encounter.

Who is this book for?

The book is primarily intended for students who are part way through a qualifying programme in social work, or who are undertaking a specialist module in adult care as part of their post-qualifying (PQ) programme. It may also be valuable for students on social policy or applied social studies degree programmes, who wish to know more about the needs of older people. It was written as a conscious demonstration of how social policy applies to social work, focusing on the experience of one particular group of service users: older people or 'elders'. It builds on introductory social policy texts you may have read, but it is not absolutely essential that you have read such texts. More importantly, by applying a social policy dimension to social work practice it will help you develop the important critical thinking skills which you must be able to demonstrate by the end of an honours degree programme in social work, or for PQ programmes at graduate certificate level.

If you intend to make social policy an important element in your undergraduate or postgraduate studies, this book will certainly help you in your quest, but it may be worth noting that there are a number of texts that offer broader introductions to social policy as an academic discipline, and you will find these listed at the end of Chapter 1. Such texts cover the theoretical ground in much greater detail than is possible here, although this text will explain some of the basic concepts and ideas used in social policy that inform social work practice. This book will help you understand how the experience of older service users is partly determined by historical and political processes. It will also help you understand how the way in which social work is practised, or social work services 'delivered', is the product of history, ideology and policy developments.

The QAA Subject Benchmarks

Clarification of the knowledge and skills you need to acquire can be found in the QAA Subject Benchmarks, and listed below you will find the specific benchmarks covered in this book. Subject Benchmarks set out expectations about standards of knowledge, skills, understanding and competence that you will be expected to attain by the end of your degree. They therefore underpin your degree course and your tutors will be looking to see if you have met the requirements of each statement. The QAA Subject Benchmarks for Social Work were published in 2008 (QAA 2008) but also relevant here are the QAA Subject Benchmarks for Social Policy (QAA 2007) which is where we start.

Social Policy Benchmarks

The Social Policy Benchmarks suggest (and for social work students it is a suggestion, for you are not aiming to attain a degree in social policy to which these benchmarks primarily relate) that students should demonstrate knowledge and understanding in the following areas.

origins and development of UK welfare institutions and the social and demographic contexts in which they have operated	Benchmark 3.2
main features of the interrelationship between social policies and differently placed communities, families and individuals	Benchmark 3.2
key concepts and theories of welfare	Benchmark 3.3
theories of the state and policy making	Benchmark 3.3
history of contemporary social problems and of social policy responses to them	Benchmark 3.3

You will find these benchmarks well covered in Chapters 2–4 of this book, which provide an overview of the development of social policy in this area. Also incorporated into all chapters are some exercises which will help you acquire the following.

well-developed descriptive skills and basic analytic skills	Benchmark 5.4
an ability to distinguish between some of the core theories, concepts and approaches in social policy	Benchmark 5.4

Social Work Benchmarks

The Social Work Benchmarks relate to the desired outcomes of an honours degree in social work, indicating both areas of knowledge and skills for social work practice. As far as knowledge is concerned, this book will most certainly help in developing understanding in the following specific areas.

5.1.1 Social work services, users and carers

2.	explanations of the links between definitional processes contributing to social differences (for example, social class, gender, ethnic differences, age, sexuality and religious belief) to the problems of inequality and differential need faced by service users
3.	the nature of social work services in a diverse society (with particular reference to concepts such as prejudice, interpersonal, institutional and structural discrimination, empowerment and anti-discriminatory practices)

5.1.2 Service delivery context

1.	the location of contemporary social work within historical, comparative and global perspectives, including European and international contexts	Chapters 2, 3, 4 and 7
2.	the changing demography and cultures of communities in which social workers will be practising	Chapters 2, 3, 4, 5 and 7, especially Chapter 5 regarding culture
3.	the complex relationships between public, social and political philosophies, policies and priorities and the organisation and practice of social work, including the contested nature of these	Chapters 2, 3, 4 for the development of these; Chapters 5 and 6 for contemporary aspects
4.	the issues and trends in modern public and social policy and their relationship to contemporary practice and service delivery in social work	Chapters 5 and 6 are all about policy and their relationship to contemporary practice, in relation to older people and service delivery in social work
5.	the significance of legislative and legal frameworks and service delivery standards (including the nature of legal authority, the application of legislation in practice, statutory accountability and tensions between statute, policy and practice)	while Chapters 3 and 4 analyse the development of legal frameworks, it is Chapters 5 and 6 that relate current legislative and legal frameworks to policy and practice
6.	the current range and appropriateness of statutory, voluntary and private agencies providing community-based, day-care, residential and other services and the organisational systems inherent within these	Chapters 5 and 6
9.	the development of personalised services, individual budgets and direct payments	this is the central theme of Chapter 6

The book is also relevant generally in these areas.

5.1.1 Social work services, service users and carers

1.	the social processes that lead to marginalisation, isolation and exclusion, and their impact on the demand for social work services
2.	explanations of the links between definitional processes contributing to social differences (for example, social class, gender, ethnic differences, age, sexuality and religious belief) to the problems of inequality and differential need faced by service users

5.1.3 Values and ethics

1.	the nature, historical evolution and application of social work values
3.	the complex relationships between justice, care and control in social welfare and the practical and ethical implications of these, including roles as statutory agents and in upholding the law in respect of discrimination

5.1.4 Social work theory

2.	the relevance of sociological perspectives to understanding societal and structural influences on human behaviour at individual, group and community levels

As far as skills are concerned, this book will mirror the importance attributed in Social Work Benchmark 4.7 to accountability, reflection, critical thinking and evaluation. The skills you should acquire by the time you graduate are specifically addressed and developed in certain chapters of this book (see next section) with the intention of enhancing your ability in the following.

learn to think logically, systematically, critically and reflectively	Benchmark 5.5.1
employ a critical understanding of human agency at the macro (societal), mezzo (organisational and community) and micro (inter and intrapersonal) levels	Benchmark 5.5.3

This book will certainly help you to do that, to relate individual circumstances to theories and explanations at different levels. Interconnecting social policy and social work enables the book to make reference to various theories and concepts that will help you to understand the position of service users and carers.

Skills development

Each chapter therefore will make explicit which particular skill or set of skills is being addressed and developed in that chapter, and for this purpose each chapter will start with a case study which is analysed during the chapter. In order to reflect the needs of students at Level 2 and Level 3 of their degree programme, the focus is on the following skills.

skill 1	demonstrating understanding and application of theoretical ideas
skill 2	comparing and contrasting different viewpoints and experiences
skill 3	relating different views to underlying philosophies or ideologies
skill 4	evaluating different perspectives and ideas
skill 5	evaluating evidence
skill 6	synthesising arguments
skill 7	reflection
skill 8	reviewing, re-evaluating and reformulating your own views

This introduction includes summaries of the content of each chapter together with an indication of the specific skill which provides a focus for the exercises in each of them. The book is intended to be interactive; that is, at various points in the discussion you will be asked to stop and engage in some kind of practical task that will enhance your learning and skills development. It is important that you allow yourself time to complete these exercises, since they will form the basis for higher-level academic work.

By way of preparation for skills development, you may find it useful to look or look again at textbooks that introduced you to the specific study skills that you need to acquire in order to do well in your studies. This book assumes that you are generally familiar with the purpose of theory, what is distinctive about academic writing, and how to begin to engage in analysis and reflection. For undergraduate students on social work qualifying programmes there are books that cover basic study skills (Walker 2008) and critical learning skills (Jones 2009) while for PQ students there are books on critical thinking such as Brown and Rutter (2008). Social policy students may find it worthwhile revisiting books such as Cottrell (2008).

As far as social work practice skills are concerned, the emphasis in this book is on the context in which social work practice takes place. The book does not aim to tell you how to deal with a particular case or a particular situation. Indeed this book is not so much about direct practice with people, so much as understanding why practice takes the particular form that it does. In this way it complements social work practice texts such as *Social Work with Older People* (Crawford and Walker 2008).

Applying policy to practice: What's in this book?

This book introduces you to some key ideas and concepts in social policy that are particularly relevant for social work and older people, at the same time developing important academic skills that will help you achieve the learning outcomes for a degree in social policy or social work. The aim of the whole book is to serve as a general introduction to social policy for people studying on social work courses, but please bear in mind that the focus on older people means that some aspects of social policy may be overlooked. For example, much has been written about what sociologists call 'moral panics' and their impact on policy, but as this has had a particular effect on social work with children, this would be better covered in a text that focused on childcare social work. Conversely, changes in the arrangements for the care of older people have been enormously influenced by marketisation, the encouragement of competition between service providers, and the shift from formal to informal or 'community' care, which some commentators say equates simply with 'family' care. So in this book considerable attention will be paid to marketisation and community care developments. Anyone practising in this field of social work would need to know about these.

Following on from this introduction, chapters in this book focus on developments in social work and social work practice with older people. All of these begin with some kind of case study, and all of them will demonstrate how a social policy analysis helps us understand the position of older people and social work issues that relate to them. Each focuses on a particular aspect of critical thinking.

In the following chapter you will be asked to unpack or analyse what appears to be a comparatively short case study in order to identify some underlying assumptions and connect these to wider structural and policy issues, issues to which we will be constantly returning later in the book. This is an important starting point in developing skills 1, 2, 3 and 4.

Chapter 2 recalls an earlier era in which social work was only just beginning to develop. Here you will be invited to compare and contrast the lived experience of older people in the Edwardian period with their experience in Britain today (skill 2, skill 7). The case studies for this chapter are drawn from some documentary evidence on the lived experience of older people before the First World War, and this is then connected to the prevailing political ideas of the time, when the government (or state) for the first time passed legislation that was intended to benefit older people. At the same time, society was segregated in the sense of consisting of well demarcated social divisions, which had the consequence of compelling some older people to enter institutions, thereby excluding them from the community. This was facilitated by a number of prevailing ideas or ideologies concerned with personal responsibility, liberalist approaches to social policy, a scientific rationalist approach to social problems, and an economic rationale for a punitive approach towards people who could not look after themselves.

Chapter 3 focuses on the major policy shift that led to the creation of the welfare state, which led to a period that some describe as the zenith of social work. Here you will be asked to connect policy developments to underlying philosophies and ideologies (skill 3, skill 4). Some legislation from that era that relates to this service-user group is still in force, for example the National Assistance Act 1948, and much of the ideology that underpinned the welfare state influenced the growth in social work and a revolution in the care of older people. Nevertheless, assumptions about social structures and the role of the family are still apparent both during this period and today, and of course there have been major demographic changes. An analysis of this helps to understand some of the challenges confronting practitioners in making arrangements to support older people today.

Chapter 4 offers an exposition of community care, both in the sense of what might be termed 'deinstitutionalisation'; that is, moving people out of institutional care and into the community, and also in terms of supporting people to continue living in the community. Here you will evaluate policy developments in the light of an understanding of underlying theory and ideology (skill 1). From a policy perspective, the key landmarks are the Griffiths Report (1988) and the introduction of internal markets in the health and social care services. Underpinning this is a move to neoclassical economic policies and the rise of the New Right. This chapter will help you to understand how markets are supposed to facilitate the delivery of services, how these relate to the fundamental notions of individual freedom, choice and the role the state, and therefore offer insights that are directly relevant to the way in which social work services are delivered today. In terms of skills, this chapter will focus on evaluation (skill 4), incorporating an assessment of the strengths and weaknesses of the free-market approach to social work and social care.

Chapter 5 is the first of three chapters that looks at some specific aspects of policy, research and contemporary social work practice. Here you will be required to assess how social policy should respond to the lived realities of particular groups of older service users (skill 5). In this chapter, the focus is on diversity in all its forms, with less on the more theoretical constructs, but still incorporating an acknowledgement of the key perspectives and ideas underpinning social policy generally. Specifically this chapter is orientated towards consideration of the challenges for social policy presented by the diversity of older people. It focuses on the challenges of responding to the needs of minority groups that share a common identity or groups who have experienced certain forms of disadvantage or oppression. The discussion incorporates references to demographic trends, since these will have a real impact on social policy. Much of the chapter draws on research concerning the needs of the older population, breaking these down into six categories which constitute the main areas of concern relating to diversity and the social position of older people. The last of these categories relates to older people as carers. This is an aspect of older people's lives that receives scant attention. Since 1995 there have been three separate Acts of Parliament about carers, and social workers are required to consider their needs in community care assessments, yet the underlying assumption appears to be that it is the older person who is the recipient, rather than the giver, of care. This carer theme is also picked up in the case study in Chapter 6. The analysis in Chapter 5 is intended to help students understand the position of different groups in Britain today directly addressing the *interrelationship between social policies and differently placed communities, families and individuals* (Social Policy Benchmark 3.2).

Chapter 6 addresses the more specific policy and practice issues of empowerment and personalisation. In the policy arena there has been a succession of Green and White papers, all of which have placed a great deal of emphasis on service user choice, organisation of responsive services (including interprofessional working) and professionals becoming facilitators and enablers rather than direct service providers. There has been a strong shift towards service users taking responsibility for commissioning and securing services themselves through direct payments. This chapter explores the background to all of this, and in doing so asks you to evaluate the merits and shortcomings of this policy (skill 4). The Social Work Benchmark statement (QAA 2008, 2.2) includes a requirement that you *learn to promote the key outcomes for adult social care services* and then makes specific reference to the White Paper *Our Health, Our Care, Our Say* (Department of Health 2006) – hence the chapter title. So in a sense this chapter is prescriptive; as social workers you are required to argue for the attainment of certain defined policy targets, so in this chapter we will look at how you might construct a response to the expressed policy intention of encouraging the empowerment of older people in this specific way (skills 6 and 8). What role does social work have in the promotion of personalisation?

Chapter 7 adopts a broader perspective, introducing some international comparisons of policy relating to care of older people, and contrasting these with developments in the UK. All of these have direct implications for practice, offering a valuable look to the future, anticipating where policy developments may be directing practice and indicating what lessons can be learned from elsewhere (skill 7, skill 8). This presents you with an opportunity to analyse at the very broadest level, to reflect on how services are constructed and delivered in the UK, and to evaluate the potential for learning from the experiences of others. You will note in this chapter some interesting similarities and differences between the UK and other countries. One common theme is the relationship between the state and the family concerning the extent to which the state should provide care, and to what extent families have responsibilities.

The final chapter attempts to bring all these strands together, connecting the theory to social policy, social policy to social work, and leaving you with a number of questions for consideration for the future. Like this Introduction it is a short chapter which adopts a different format without any specific skills related exercise, although there is a separate study skills summary of what you should have learned by the time you reach the end of the book.

Thus each subsequent chapter begins with some kind of case study which is used as a focus for a discussion of social policy and its connections to social work practice. Needless to say all cases are fictional and hypothetical. The structure of each chapter varies slightly, although each introduces specific concepts used in social policy. Included within each chapter are some study activities, usually involving reflecting on an extract from a social policy text or thinking about the connections between social policy and social work practice. At various points in later chapters you are asked to consider the implications of relevant research. You will find this useful for any preparation you may have to undertake as part of your course including planning for a dissertation, and it also connects to the Department of Health requirement that social work should seek to be evidence-based; that is, good practice should be built on the outcomes of good research. In addition there is a guidance for further reading, and it is important to make use of this if your degree course includes assignments that are specifically social policy assignments. For it is impossible in a text of this length to do full justice to the more theoretical arguments used by social policy analysts, nor is it possible to enter into the more philosophical and theoretical debates, such as those that centre on postmodernism. However, the hope is that you will be stimulated to move on to an exploration of those kinds of ideas and above all the ambition is that, by the time you have finished reading this book, you will be much clearer about how social policy has a direct impact on social work practice, at least in one area of social work practice.

1 Why Do Social Work Practitioners Need to Know About Social Policy?

Robert Johns

Achieving a Social Work or Social Policy Degree

The exercises and content in this chapter will focus on

- ⊙ skill 1 demonstrating understanding and application of theoretical ideas
- ⊙ skill 4 evaluating different perspectives and ideas

In addition its content is particularly relevant to the following Social Work Subject Benchmarks.

5.1.1 the social processes that lead to marginalisation, isolation and exclusion, and their impact on the demand for social work services
explanations of the links between definitional processes contributing to social differences (for example, social class, gender, ethnic differences, age, sexuality and religious belief) to the problems of inequality and differential need faced by service users
5.1.4 the relevance of sociological perspectives to understanding societal and structural influences on human behaviour at individual, group and community levels

---

Introduction

In the introduction to this book you were told that it was about social work and social policy. Its aim is to demonstrate how social policy can help us understand the position of older people in Britain today, and also helps us to understand why social work practice takes the form that it does. So let's start with a demonstration, incorporating development of some of the core skills which it is hoped you will acquire by reading through this book.

The primary emphasis in this chapter is on connecting theoretical ideas (in this case political theory or policy) to practice. There is no better way of doing this than starting with an analysis of a case study, which of course is why every chapter in this book starts in this way. The case study is intended as the focus for a discussion of social policy.

Applying policy to practice

> **CASE STUDY**
>
> Stella Fordham, aged 55, cares full-time for her mother Beatrice who is 80. Beatrice has dementia. She is no longer able to look after herself, and is unsafe if left on her own. Stella is now in a position of doing virtually everything for her mother, who is becoming increasingly frail. They live together in Beatrice's house, which is in urgent need of repairs to the central heating system; the house is rented.

So looking at this case study, what have you noticed so far?

> **Critical thinking exercise 1.1**
>
> With the limited information you have about the case study, what factors do you think are significant? What else do you need to know?
>
> Note you are not being asked what you would do, but what information is important in any kind of analysis of Stella and her mother's situation.

There are number of factors you might have identified quite quickly but at this stage there is no way of telling which is more important than the other. So let's just list them in no particular order.

- Both people in the case study are female.
- One person (Stella) is the carer.
- The carer's responsibilities and duties amount, in her view, to almost full-time care.
- The person being cared for (Beatrice) has a health condition which affects her ability to live independently.
- Beatrice appears to have lost an element of control over her own life.
- Beatrice is a tenant and the house needs improving.

Thus far we have factual information. Now let's add to it some interpretations and indications of further information we require for an understanding of the case. We might want to know:

- if there are other relatives and how much family and community support there is;
- whether Stella was working and gave up a job in order to take on full-time carer responsibilities;
- if Stella is happy in her role as carer, or feels she needs more support and whether assumptions were made that Stella should be the principal or sole carer;

- whether a formal diagnosis of dementia has been made rather than assumptions being made about certain patterns of behaviour in older people;
- whether it would be right to describe the person being cared for as vulnerable because of her health and dependence on the carer and what system there is in place to protect her;
- what services there are to promote the well-being of vulnerable older people;
- the legal position of Stella as regards the tenancy of the property once Beatrice dies, and what can be done about the heating issue.

There are probably lots of other pieces of information we would like to have, but this will be enough to be going on with for the moment, since there is plenty of material here to suggest that there is a much broader context which it is important to understand. Every single one of the questions we might want to ask is not just a practice question, but has a policy or political aspect to it. For example, taking each of the points listed above in turn:

Exploring family and community support will inevitably tell us something about family structures, and also about the general arrangements to address the needs of vulnerable older people and support for carers. It may well be that there are relatives, but they live at a considerable distance, possibly abroad. What is the impact of family structure on older people and their carers? Do people within families feel they have obligations to each other or is it the case that some people feel they have such duties, or possibly are made to feel that they do? Do the arrangements for community support reflect assumptions about the role of the family and individuals within the family, or to put it another way, to what extent does the society in which Stella and Beatrice live accept responsibility for vulnerable adults? In some societies, caring may be seen as a fulfilling and worthwhile task, whereas in others the status of the carer is less positive. Of particular importance for social workers is the challenge of securing support for older people and those who care for them: how easy or difficult is this? Assumptions about who should be the carer may well reflect gender assumptions, so here we need to explore gender divisions and need to have an understanding of how men and women's roles can be differently perceived.

Alongside assumptions about families, there may also be assumptions about economic activity; that is, there may be an assumption that people 'work for a living'. This applies both to older people themselves and to their carers. If that is the case, what then of people who are not 'economically active' but do in fact work full-time in the sense that they care full-time? How are they perceived? How does the 'system' address their needs?

The question of diagnosis of dementia is not an absolute; that is, there may have to be judgements made about the extent to which behaviour can be explained by a medical condition. Given that assessments invariably depend on interpretation of behaviour, the question arises about the extent to which assumptions may be made, and here we move on to ageism rather than gender assumptions.

Protecting vulnerable people raises a whole host of issues concerned with people's rights to self-determination, and the balance between protection and interfering in people's private lives. The extent to which the state feels under an obligation to intervene depends, critically, on assumptions by policymakers about the general relationship between individuals and the state, and of course the definition of what is 'private'. Social work practitioners must understand what they can and cannot do, but this is determined by what the law allows them to do. In order to understand this, it is crucial to understand the social policy dimension, along with competing theories about the state and the individual. This may also help us understand differences between social arrangements for protection of particular groups: for example, why protection of children is accorded greater weight and thus more state intervention than the protection of vulnerable older people. The extent to which services are available to promote the well-being of vulnerable older people also depends on this kind of understanding. In addition, provision of services must inevitably relate to the financial resources made available. Accessibility of financial resources in turn depends on a whole series of political decisions, such as use of taxation (fiscal policy) and the extent to which the government controls the economy and service providers. Protection of vulnerable older people is influenced by nearly all of the factors already cited, but in addition policymakers would need to decide about where the legal responsibility for co-ordinating a system for protection might lie, and how much power to delegate to social workers and others. Who decides?

An objective observer might be potentially alarmed at the implications for Stella of not being a tenant herself, but to what extent is this a social work issue? Should social workers be concerned about housing? Where does the role of the social worker begin and end? All of these are determined by various social and political forces, which can be analysed through an examination of the role of social work through the twentieth century. That century saw the transformation of social work from an activity based on charity to a period when social work was a major component of the welfare state and then latterly part of the reformulated welfare system with its 'mixed economy of care'.

From all of this you can see that a comparatively short case scenario description has raised a whole number of very broad issues that will have a direct or indirect impact on social work practice. In the Introduction we explained what this book is about, and how each chapter addresses these broad issues. The remainder of this chapter returns to the case study and introduces you to some of the ways in which studying social policy helps social workers to understand the issues and challenges of everyday practice. This will begin to incorporate the core skills listed above. The broader issues raised by the case study were in brief:

- the role of the family;
- the economy and the individual;
- ageism;
- deciding priorities and the role of the state;
- the role of social workers.

We now look at each of these in turn.

The role of the family

In the analysis of the case study above, our first point concerned the family. To what extent do family members feel they have obligations towards each other?

Critical thinking exercise 1.2: Family and community support

There have been a number of studies of changing family relationships and the extent to which people feel responsibility for the care of elders within their own families. Take one example from the following and then complete the tasks listed below.

Charles, N., Davies, C. and Harris, C. (2004) *Family Formation and Kin Relationships: 40 Years of Social Change* (available at www.swan.ac.uk/sssid/Research/Res%20 -%20Sociology.htm; also via ESRC website, www.esrcsocietytoday.ac.uk)

Finch, J. and Mason, J. (1993) *Negotiating Family Responsibilities.* London: Taylor and Francis

Millar, J. (2003) Social Policy and Family Policy, in Alcock, P., Erskine, A. and May, M. (2008): *The Student's Companion to Social Policy.* Oxford: Blackwell

List the key points that emerge from this research or policy analysis.

Note down what you think are the implications for social work.

The purpose of this exercise was not just to introduce you to research which may have an impact on social work practice or social policy, but also to introduce you to a study skill related to accessing high-quality research or academic analysis, summarising it and exploring its implications. As you progress through your course, this skill will gain in importance.

One of the points you ought to have noted is the extent to which family members feel obligated, at least to some extent, to care for their elders. This obligation may not be as deep as that felt towards children, and indeed it is not underpinned by the law to the same extent as the obligation to care for children in the Children Act 1989, but it is nevertheless there. One other point you may have noted concerns gender, namely that women feel under a stronger obligation than men to offer care, an obligation that may include feeling obliged to support people who are not direct blood relatives; for example, women who feel a duty towards a former partner's mother.

This does not tell us how to respond to the needs of this particular family in this situation, rather it helps us to analyse their situation. It is important to remember that social policy is not prescriptive; it does not tell social workers what to do. Instead it helps social workers to relate the issues that challenge a particular family to the wider social context. Why does Stella feel under an obligation to be a full-time carer? Is this common? What social and political forces encourage women in particular to think that they have these obligations? Your reading should already have made you think about these issues.

The economy and the individual

Going along with the current assumption that an older person is one whose age is 65 or above, the one distinguishing feature older people possess compared with the rest of the adult population is that the majority do not 'work for a living'. For the most part, older people are retired. As we will see in Chapter 2, the whole concept of retirement is not universal, for in Britain a hundred years ago many people worked until they became physically unable to do so, and indeed it was commonplace for people to come to the end of their lives when they were still in full-time employment. One of the remarkable innovations of the first decade of the twentieth century was the introduction of pensions (discussed further in Chapter 2), so that those who contributed to a national insurance scheme no longer had to work after a certain age. This would naturally lead us to question whether lack of economic activity has an effect on the status of older people, and may help to explain why older people can be perceived to be 'useless' or a 'burden'.

Likewise we might ask whether the same applies to the carer, and this is obviously very relevant to Stella in our case study. Despite the fact that carers are often unpaid, their work can absorb more hours than those of people who are in 'full-time' employment. Yet different perceptions may apply because of the position of the care within the economy. Carers can be disadvantaged in two respects: firstly and most obviously their day-to-day caring responsibilities can be burdensome, but secondly they can lose out in relation to their position in a competitive employment market.

Critical thinking exercise 1.3: Economic activity and support for carers

The following short extracts come from an article based on research commissioned by the Department for Work and Pensions. The article appeared in the journal *Social Policy and Administration*. If you possibly can, do get hold of the original article: Arksey, H. and Glendinning, C. (2008) Combining Work and Care: Carers' Decision-making in the Context of Competing Policy Pressures. *Social Policy and Administration*, 42 (1): 1–18.

As you are reading through this article, carry out the following activities.

- List the key points that emerge from this research or policy analysis
- Note down what you think are the implications for social work and social policy.
- Take note of the way in which the authors present their work.

Note: the references that appear in the Research Extract that follows do not appear in the references in this book. If you want to see the sources cited you will need to consult the original article itself.

Research extract: Combining work and care

The majority of working-age carers, especially those providing care for 20 hours or more per week, are female (Maher and Green 2002). Demand for labour has resulted in a situation where women in their forties and fifties are being targeted by government and employers to enter and/or remain in the labour market (DWP 2005; Mooney and Statham 2002). At the same time, more care demands are being made upon older women (and men) as the likelihood of taking on caregiving responsibilities increases with age: in Britain, the peak age for starting a caring role is between 45 and 64 years (Hirst 2002).

Combining work with care is known to be difficult (Phillips 1994, 1995; Arksey 2002; Seddon et al. 2004). Social services support can be important to help carers fulfil the two activities (Carers National Association 1999; Seddon et al. 2004; Stiell et al. 2006). Carers may be helped through direct service provision, as well as indirectly through services aimed at the person supported but which also substitute for the carer's presence (Twigg 1992; Pickard 2004). Services that are perceived as inflexible, unreliable or of poor quality can discourage carers from working and caring (Phillips et al. 2002; Pickard 2004).

Recent research suggests there are business and social benefits for employers who support staff with caring responsibilities (Yeandle et al. 2006). Flexibility in the workplace is essential to enable such individuals to reconcile work and care (DH 1999; Phillips 2002; Seddon et al. 2004). Carers who take advantage of flexible working arrangements such as part-time hours, job share or working from home may nonetheless experience negative professional, financial and personal consequences (Anderson 2003; Heitmueller and Inglis 2004; Stiell et al. 2006). Some carers cease paid work because of caring (Arber and Ginn 1995), but the evidence suggests that most manage to combine the two activities (Parker 1990; Glendinning 1992; Joshi 1995).

For the first time, the UK 2001 Census asked a question about unpaid caregiving for relatives, friends or neighbours. The evidence showed the regional variations in the prevalence of unpaid caregiving, including the relationships between different prevalence rates and different types of labour markets (Buckner and Yeandle 2006; Young et al. 2006). The Census also showed that in England and Wales working carers are more likely to be unqualified, and less likely to hold university degrees, than other people in employment (Buckner and Yeandle 2006). Furthermore, people with caregiving responsibilities are concentrated in lower-level jobs.

This extract from a much longer article highlights very concisely the economic position of carers who appear to experience a number of employment-related disadvantages as a result of taking on caring responsibilities. Some of these you may have anticipated: losing out on career development, ending up being less qualified than other people, and in some cases being forced to disengage from the employment market altogether. There is also the inescapable fact the majority of carers are women who face the pressure of feeling obliged to be carers yet at the same time being encouraged by government to enter employment.

So how might this evidence have an impact on social work practice and social policy? Firstly it points to the importance of providing support, and in employment practical arrangements to facilitate working. Flexible working hours, the ability to work from home, and similar arrangements are important; the policy to encourage this became formalised into legislation, the Work and Families Act 2006. At the same time it is clear that carers will need support in the actual caring task. It is for this reason that there are a number of pieces of legislation that accord carers rights in addition to the rights of the older person themselves. In social policy terms this has taken the form of the Carers (Recognition and Services) Act 1995, the Carers and Disabled Children Act 2000 and the Carers (Equal Opportunities) Act 2004, which between them offer carers the right to a comprehensive assessment of their needs. Financially, support might take the form of carers' allowances as compensation for loss of earning power created by caring responsibilities: in the UK this takes the form of the non-contributory Carers Allowance.

What did you notice about the way in which the article was written? Apart from the fact that it makes quite a number of points in a very short space of time, each of those points is actually supported by evidence, that is we are told where we can find confirmation of what the authors are saying. If you want to know exactly where this evidence lies, you will have to go back to the original article and look at the list of references at the end; by now you should be familiar with the system in your own university for accessing articles such as this in refereed journals. The style in which they are presented is the Harvard referencing style where there is reference to the author and year only in the text, with full references at the end. This avoids the danger of references being too disruptive in the text, yet does make it clear that there is supporting evidence. This should give you a pointer to the way in which essays and assignments need to be written at second and third level of degree courses. Those paragraphs cited above offer a very useful model.

Not surprisingly, having presented the evidence from other authors and researchers, and combining this with their own research on carers' attempts to combine work and care, the authors can present persuasive and convincing arguments. In this particular research the conclusions include the following:

 Irrespective of geography, the future supply of carers is likely to depend increasingly upon people's ability to combine work and caregiving responsibilities. If the government wants to move signifcant numbers of carers back into work, a wide range of policies will be required to support them. Such policies need to recognize the diversity of carers.

Arksey and **Glendinning** (2008: 15)

Ageism

Another aspect of the case study identified earlier was that of potential ageism, that is assumptions made about older people, usually negative. There is a fuller discussion of the definition of ageism in Crawford and Walker (2008) on pages 10–11.

In essence ageism reflects overall assumptions about the role of older people in society, and inevitably this changes over time. The way in which social policy develops naturally reflects this. There will be clear evidence of this in Chapter 2 where policy in the Edwardian period directly reflected prevailing ideologies generally. This is true also in Chapter 3 yet here a very different view of older people features, one that is enshrined in universalist welfare provision, while in Chapter 4 the emphasis changes again. We are going to defer a full exploration of these differences to those chapters but here you are invited to reflect on the way in which social policy is bound to react to a broader approach to ageing generally, and older people in particular. It is not possible to get much broader than the international, so at that level it may be worth thinking about the following extract from an article that analyses the 'age shift' as it describes it; that is, changing attitudes towards older people as evidenced in changes in social policy and the adult life discourse.

Literature extract: The age shift

Should anyone doubt the sea change that has occurred, they need only compare two statements, 20 years apart, which stand as attempts to summarise contemporary thinking on the nature of old age and the contribution of older people to wider society.

In 1982, the First World Assembly on Ageing was held in Vienna. The Vienna statement underlined three factors that will increasingly impinge upon population structures by 2025. These include: a marked increase in the numbers of people over 60 and over 80 years old, of which the largest proportion will be women, that both developed and developing nations will be effected and that policy will have to change significantly 'during the first quarter of the 21st Century'. The Assembly concluded that:

> Measures for the optimum utilisation of the wisdom and expertise of elderly individuals will be considered ... the human race is characterised by a long childhood and by a long old age. Throughout history this has enabled older persons to educate the younger and pass on values to them, this role has ensured man's survival and progress ... A longer life provides humans with an opportunity to examine their lives in retrospect, to correct some of their mistakes, to get closer to the truth and to achieve a different understanding of the sense and value of their actions.

> (United Nations, 1982, p. 1.B)

▶

Vienna's final statement may be seen in retrospect to illustrate a relatively gentle view of ageing, with an emphasis on reflection, wisdom, a sense of summing up and benign disengagement. It is typical of that historical period and echoes the work of Erik Erikson among others, in focussing on a generative relationship to younger age-groups and the transmission of life experience. It also recognises that there may be significant differences that mark out the priorities of this from other parts of the adult lifecourse.

While the demographic projections of 1982 are undisputed, in 2002 a Second World Assembly on Ageing (this time held in Madrid) shows how a very different vision of later life had taken hold, best exemplified by Article 10. Here:

> the potential of older persons is a powerful basis for future development. This enables society to rely increasingly on the skills, experience and wisdom of older persons, not only to take the lead in their own betterment but also to participate actively in that of society as a whole.

(United Nations, 2002, p. 2)

The form of social inclusion envisaged by the two statements is therefore very different. One appears as a personal task looking backwards via a sifting of accrued experience, the second privileges the application of particular skills in the here and now, as a springboard for future aspirations, based around continued work activities. By 2002, there appear to be significantly fewer qualities that are distinctive to later life and significantly greater similarity between adult age groups.

Biggs S., Phillipson C., Money A-M. and **Leach R**. (2006) The Age Shift: Observations on Social Policy, Ageism and the Dynamics of the Adult Lifecourse. *Journal of Social Work Practice*, 20 (3): 239–250.

The United Nations quotations in this article are from the report of the First (1982) and Second (2002) World Assembly on Ageing.

Critical thinking exercise 1.4: Thinking about changing perceptions

Looking at this extract from this thought-provoking article, what sorts of social policy would you associate with the ideology demonstrated in the 1982 United Nations statement?

What sorts of social policy would you associate with the ideology demonstrated in the 2002 United Nations statement?

You could legitimately come up with a number of different answers to this, but clearly in relation to the 2002 view you can see that this will gear policies more towards employment enhancing provision and away from the 1982 view, which almost encourages a long, reflective holiday! The point about the exercise is that analysing policy unmasks underlying assumptions or views of older people and of course, conversely, a conceptual change will have implications for policy. Assumptions that over-65s are dependent and really rather a liability can easily lead to grudging provision of services. Yet at the same time the emphasis on rights to work and encouragement for people to work beyond retirement can unwittingly carry the assumption that people must carry on being 'productive' and those who choose not to will therefore be stigmatised. This leads neatly into consideration of the relationship between perceptions of older people, their role in society and the economy.

Deciding priorities and the role of the state

Picking up on issue 4 identified in the case study analysis earlier in the chapter, the discussion now turns to the relationship between the individual and the state. This is a key determinant in social policy, focusing on the extent to which the state should play a role in people's lives. This is a really important question, and it would be no exaggeration to say that scarcely a day goes by without practitioners and policymakers having to think about the exact relationship between the state and individual. In order to make this more real in social work terms, you may find a model put forward by Dickens (2010) helpful. This is what he calls the 'social policy triangle'.

Literature extract: the social policy triangle

Extract from Dickens (2010) adapted

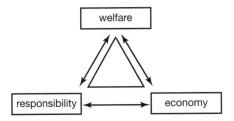

Figure 1.1: The social policy triangle

We can say that the overriding objective of social policy in Western, democratic nations with capitalist economic systems, and its overriding challenge, is to balance three demands — to ensure the welfare of citizens, to promote

---

the values of individual responsibility and family autonomy, and to uphold economic freedom and prosperity ...

The tension between welfare and economy is that high-quality social services are expensive. If the services are provided by the state, then that will mean a high tax bill — but individuals and businesses on the whole do not like to pay high taxes. The fear of politicians and policymakers is that if taxation is too high, businesses will move their factories and offices to other countries, where wages and taxes are lower. In our globalised world, it seems easier than ever. On the other hand, defenders of public services such as health, education and pensions argue that they support the economy by producing a skilled and healthy workforce. More than that, they give people a sense of social and financial security, which builds a general sense of well-being in society.

The main tension between welfare and responsibility is that that some say overly generous provision from the state undermines individual responsibility — it discourages people from saving for their old age, it weakens family ties because people no longer feel an obligation to help their relatives ('someone else will do it'), and it reduces people's dynamism by removing the need to 'get on', making life too soft and too dull. On the other hand, defenders of social services argue that most people who need help do so not because they are lazy or irresponsible, but because their needs — financial, emotional, intellectual, physical and social — are so great. Maybe they do not have families to help, or their needs are so demanding that their families cannot cope. A bit of timely help would enable some to resume self-responsibility. Others will need longer-term support, and it should be accepted as society's responsibility to provide that.

The relationship between responsibility and the economy is that, for most people, the primary way of being responsible for oneself and one's family is to work, to earn money. Welfare sceptics argue that social services make life too easy and too expensive, undermining responsibility and the economy. Supporters argue that they give the vital help people need in times of trouble, and more than that have a positive role in building up a skilled, responsible workforce and a thriving market for goods and services.

Dickens (2010: 29)

The next exercise asks you to use this extract as a way of thinking about and categorising different sets of ideas.

> **Critical thinking exercise 1.5:** Thinking about the role of the state in people's lives
>
> Building on Dickens' exposition of contrasting views, can you think of ways of classifying them into groups? For example, do you think it likely that people who believe that taxes are too high also believe that people should show greater responsibility for meeting their own needs? If so, what other ideas are likely to be in common with those beliefs?
>
> Draw up a system of grouping different ideas together in order to produce some kind of classification.

Classification, looking for commonalities, is an important skill since it is the first step towards a systematic analysis. Identifying common ground makes it easier to explore differences and, crucially, facilitates an evaluation of the merits of particular approaches. How consistent are they? How coherent? How persuasive?

One obvious way of doing this would be labelling them as the general beliefs or values of one particular political party, so you may have ended up linking a group of beliefs about the positive role of the welfare state with the Labour Party. Conversely you may have associated many of the ideas connected with personal responsibility with Conservative Party thinking, but this is actually a limited way of classifying those beliefs. The major weakness of this approach is that political parties are constantly shifting their positions over time. A quick analysis of policy statements from the Labour government from 1997 would yield many references to notions of personal responsibility and encouraging people to work and save in order to provide for themselves. Political parties are not consistent and, of course, they come and go. In the Edwardian period the Liberal Party was a key player, but is no longer so. Also a classification of this kind would be very specific to Britain. Such a classification would have serious limitations, and is therefore not generally used by social policy academics.

Instead we need to address these issues at a higher, more generalised level. There are a number of options here, and we can relate these to the social policy triangle.

- On the responsibility side, there are different views that reflect competing ideologies. In Chapter 2 you will encounter a dominant liberalism which argues that people are fundamentally responsible for themselves and therefore the state should play a minimal role in individuals' lives. In Chapter 3 this is exchanged for a different conceptualisation of freedom whereby people are provided with sufficient resources for the state to enable them to engage in society as free and (almost) equal citizens. In Chapter 4 liberalism is reasserted in a new ('neo') form: neo-liberalism, otherwise known as the New Right.

- On the economic side, the Edwardian period in Chapter 2 starts with a fundamental belief in a free market economy, with an expectation that everyone works, although that is beginning to be challenged by the introduction of pensions for older people. In the post-second world war period economic thinking takes a different turn, centring on the theories of Keynes, who promoted government intervention in the economy. In Chapter 4 this gives way to monetarism, a reassertion of the belief in free market forces operating either within the economy as a whole or else within sectors, e.g. with social services commissioned on a competitive bid basis.
- Thirdly, welfare can be classified according to the forms it takes in different countries and in different times. In a way such a classification system is bound to straddle the political and the economic, but may nevertheless be useful as it can also take on board important cultural differences that exist in different countries. Such a classification in the form of a typology was put forward by Esping-Andersen (1990) and is widely used in comparative social policy to explore commonalities and differences when analysing social policy in various countries. This typology will be used in Chapter 7.

Where does the social worker's role begin and end?

At this point you may be wondering how all this helps us to understand the position of Stella in our case study. The answer is simply that unpacking the core beliefs or theories that underpin social policy helps us understand the extent to which social workers can legitimately be involved in people's lives at a given time. Let's demonstrate this by posing two very specific questions.

Critical thinking exercise 1.6: What should be the role of the social worker?

In the case study, should the social worker contact the person or company who owns the house that Beatrice rents?

Should the social worker fill in the application form for Carer's Allowance on Stella's behalf?

Think about these questions for a few minutes, not just in terms of practice but also as regards thinking that lies behind that practice.

Many experienced social workers in the UK would, if they were truthful, answer 'no' to both questions. Indeed some would say: why on earth would they do that?

As regards the house and the heating, many would say that this was the responsibility of Beatrice and Stella between them to approach the owners and negotiate what could be done about the heating and also about Stella becoming a co-tenant with her mother. Only if there were technical or legal problems would there be a potential role for a social worker or advocate. It does not matter how precisely we address this, but what matters more at this stage is that you can now see that the answer to a practice dilemma is only the surface of a debate always simmering underneath about the responsibility of the individual, the role of welfare agents, and the economic system that undergirds it. In a state-controlled economy the status of the tenant would be secure and efficient central heating the right of all who needed it, so in that context the social worker would play a major role in advocating, indeed might be the only means of securing services. In a totally free market economy in which housing is privately owned, pressurising the owner to upgrade the heating might result in a notice to quit — scarcely the desired outcome. Thus the broader context within which practice operates must be understood.

Similar but not identical arguments apply to the issue of the Carer's Allowance. Many would argue that filling in a form for someone who has not asked you to do so undermines individual responsibility and is profoundly disempowering. Yet few would refuse to help, directly or indirectly, if asked to do so. Deciding at what point to do things 'for' people is not a matter of individual social worker choice or whim; behind it lies a complex set of interwoven ideas about personal responsibility, the role of the state in welfare and again economic considerations: should entitlement to a Carer's Allowance be dependent on demonstrating loss of income? Should the allowance be available to carers who were not in paid employment prior to becoming full-time carers? While the answers to some of these questions are not determined by social workers as individuals, quite often how social workers carry out their tasks is influenced by their own beliefs about the answers to these questions. It would not be appropriate to pursue the practice questions here, but suffice it to say that it should now be patently clear why it is argued that the role of social work is inextricably linked to social policy.

Chapter Summary

In the second half of this chapter you have been introduced to some important concepts that will help you understand social policy. By analysing a particular case study, we have been able to say something about the extent to which family members feel an obligation towards each other, the connections between economics and people's position in society, the way in which older people are perceived, gender assumptions about who provides care, ageism, the relationship between the individual and the state, and finally about social work itself. During this discussion we have covered a number of concepts and principles. These include:

- the importance of using sociological research to help understand people's lived experiences;

- the important role economics plays in influencing social policy and the way people are expected to make arrangements for themselves and their welfare;
- assumptions about gender roles;
- assumptions about the role of older people in society with reference to ageism;
- structure and agency; that is, the role of the individual and the extent to which they are expected to be responsible for themselves;
- ways of classifying different approaches to social policy;
- how the role of the social worker can only be understood by reference to social policy and the theories and principles that underscore it.

It is important to ensure at this stage that you understand what all of these mean, for the rest of the book builds on these and introduces you to key ideas in social policy. If you are at all unsure it would be advisable to go back and re-read the relevant parts of this chapter.

In the next chapter we begin our analysis of the development of social work in its social policy context by examining a period before social work became a welfare state function. The Edwardian period saw the introduction of the first pensions in Britain, and this marked an important change in thinking about the role of the state in people's lives. Not surprisingly, you will discover that at this time there were specific dominant views about responsibility, the economy and the role of welfare services. It is a fascinating period, in some ways very different from our own, yet in other respects some ideas important at that time continue to be important today.

Further reading

Crawford, K. and Walker, J. (2008) *Social Work and Older People* (2nd edition). Exeter: Learning Matters.
This is the definitive basic social work text on social work practice with older people.

Social policy texts
Dickens, J. (2010) *Social Work and Social Policy: An Introduction.* Abingdon: Routledge.
This is one of the few social policy books written specifically for social work students and is very accessible, being intended for students who have limited previous knowledge of social policy.
Alcock, P., Erskine, A., and May, M. (2008) *The Student's Companion to Social Policy* (3rd edition). Oxford: Blackwell.
or

Baldock, J., Manning, N. and Vickerstaff, S. (2007) *Social Policy* (3rd edition). Oxford: Oxford University Press.

or

Hill, M. and Irving, Z. (2009) *Understanding Social Policy* (8th edition). Oxford: Wiley-Blackwell.

All of these three textbooks are good, sound, comprehensive basic social policy texts. They differ in style rather than substance so the choice really depends on individual preference, but it is certainly worthwhile having one as a constant reference point.

Skills texts

Cottrell, S. (2008) *The Study Skills Handbook* (3rd edition). Basingstoke: Palgrave.

This is an excellent, well established basic academic study skills book. It was written very much with students new to higher education in mind. Contains lots of useful exercises.

Jones, S. (2009) *Critical Learning for Social Work Students.* Exeter: Learning Matters.

This is an ideal companion for this book as it explains how to develop critical skills needed for higher level academic work. It does this by using a range of examples which are explored in much more detail than is possible in this book. There is even a worked example on older people and poverty in Chapter 1.

Walker, H. (2008) *Studying for Your Social Work Degree.* Exeter: Learning Matters.

An example-rich guide to the skills needed for successful studies at undergraduate level.

Brown, K. and Rutter, L. (2008) *Critical Thinking for Social Work* (2nd edition). Exeter: Learning Matters.

Focuses on needs of post-qualifying students and provides guidance on developing critical skills for that level.

2 Before the Welfare State: **Older People in the Edwardian Era**

Robert Johns

Achieving a Social Work or Social Policy Degree

This chapter will help you begin to develop critical thinking skills. Exercises in this chapter will focus on

- ☉ skill 2 comparing and contrasting different viewpoints and experiences
- ☉ skill 3 relating different views to underlying philosophies or ideologies
- ☉ skill 7 reflection

It is highly relevant to the following Social Policy Benchmarks.

3.2 origins and development of UK welfare institutions and the social and demographic contexts in which they have operated
theories of the state and policymaking

3.3 history of contemporary social problems and of social policy responses to them

In addition its content is particularly relevant to the following Social Work Subject Benchmarks.

5.1.1 explanations of the links between definitional processes contributing to social differences to the problems of inequality and differential need faced by service users
the nature of social work services in a diverse society

5.1.3 the complex relationships between justice, care and control in social welfare and the practical and ethical implications of these

Introduction

Despite what Henry Ford said – 'history is bunk' – history is actually very important in people's lives. People will of course have their own personal histories which form their own identities and for older people in particular their early life history becomes of greater significance as they move towards the end of their own lives. In terms of social policy and social work, history is important for what it tells us about the way in which society has addressed the needs of older people in past times and what we can learn from that experience. In this chapter we are going to examine the life experience, very briefly, of older people in Britain before the First World War, the Edwardian era 1901–1910. The chapter then goes on to look at the way in which policies began to change at this time in order to allow for a larger role for the state in contributing to old people's welfare, which raised all sorts of issues at the time reflecting the prevailing political ideologies. The chapter explores what these were and suggest ways in which they may have influenced policy right up until the present day.

CASE STUDY

Old age in Edwardian times

The following is an extract from The Edwardians *(Thompson 1992)*

Three-generational homes were very rare outside the textile and pottery districts, where married women more commonly continued in industrial work. Nevertheless, once grandchildren had been born, many grandparents could provide practical help in child care, especially if they lived near by. A close bond might continue, particularly between grandmother and daughter. But before long, especially in the years before the introduction of old age pensions, the need for help would be reversed. Although occupational pensions had begun to spread, they were only normal among civil service and railway office staff: altogether, only one man in twenty was covered. So Edwardian workers kept on as long as they had strength, typically shifting to worse-paid less skilled jobs as watchmen, roadmen or carrying out minor repairs. Once past this, the ageing couple would slip helplessly towards extreme poverty. They had reached a stage at which once again, as in childhood, the inequalities of age overshadowed those of sex.

Because of the higher death rates of the early twentieth century, it was in fact only a minority of Edwardians who lived long enough to meet this crisis of old age. Men especially were more likely to die before their mid-sixties. Altogether a mere 5 per cent of the national population was aged over sixty-five, in contrast to 15 per cent today. Of those who lived, half were widowed; and if Rowntree's information for York is typical, nearly half shared a household with their children or grandchildren, generally unmarried – in other words, they still had descendants in their own homes. Married children would often give infirm parents practical help, but rarely money, and they were also reluctant to take them into their own homes. There was a long-standing belief, exceptionally emphasized in English culture, that the older generation should if possible retain their own independent households. Rowntree found that a quarter took in paid lodgers, and there were also poor inner city streets where some widows clustered together. Nevertheless nearly one in ten was reduced to living in the workhouse. It is true that old people in the workhouses were generally either ill, or had lost contact with relatives. But by the age of seventy, one Edwardian in five was a pauper; and of those who lived to seventy-five, almost one in three. An old person's chance of actually dying in the workhouse in the years before a national health service was still higher.

The rough diet of the workhouse, a rhythm of broth, boiled bacon and dumplings, was good enough by the meagre standards of the Edwardian poor. But the old, since they were not given false teeth, could hardly eat it; and the price of the diet was the degrading regimentation shown in George Sims's picture of a workhouse dinner from *Living London*. Even as a visitor, the East London socialist George Lansbury was so shocked by his first encounter with the workhouse that he gave a large part of his political life to improving its conditions:

> My first visit to the workhouse was a memorable one. Going down the narrow lane, ringing the bell, waiting while an official with a not too pleasant face looked through a grating to see who was there, and hearing his unpleasant voice – of course, he did not know me – made it easy for me to understand why the poor dreaded and hated these places, and made me in a flash realize how all these prison or bastille sort of surroundings were organized for the purpose of making self-respecting, decent people endure any suffering rather than enter.

> It was not necessary to write up the words 'Abandon hope all ye who enter here'. Officials, receiving ward, hard forms, whitewashed walls, keys dangling at the waist of those who spoke to you, huge books for name, history, etc., searching, and then being stripped and bathed in a communal tub, and the final crowning indignity of being dressed in clothes which had been worn by lots of other people, hideous to look at, ill-fitting and coarse – everything possible was done to inflict mental and moral degradation.

> The place was clean: brass knobs and floors were polished, but of goodwill, kindliness, there was none.

> It was in such a setting that an ordinary Edwardian who had lived his full life span might end his days. It was perhaps best for men that they died first.

Thompson (1992: 69–70)

This case study is rather different from a conventional case study, in that it looks at a group of people who lived in the UK in the first decade of the twentieth century. It refers to one of the original pieces of social research, carried out by Rowntree (see below), which offered a comprehensive survey of poverty and was to some extent influential in changing social policy so that it became more sympathetic towards the needs of the poor. The specific aspect of the lived experience of older people that may well strike you as particularly harsh is the workhouse, and the first part of the chapter looks at some of the justifications for such a harsh regime, connecting these to some social policy concepts introduced in the first chapter, and introducing you to some new ones. However, before we do this, look back at the case-study example and then answer the questions in the next exercise.

Critical thinking exercise 2.1

Compare the experience of older people in Edwardian times described above with what you know about the experience of older people in Britain today.

What are the key differences? What are the similarities?

The first and most striking difference, of course, is that there were far fewer older people in Britain a hundred years ago compared with today: 5 per cent of the population compared with more than 15 per cent (the 2001 census data suggests the current figure would be 18 per cent, with 1.9 per cent being over 85). Consequently three-generational households were rare, but some families benefited from the care a grandparent could offer. However, it looks as though older people became dependent much sooner, and certainly this would have been true in regards to financial support as only those in a relatively select few occupations had pensions. It has been estimated that 60 per cent of Edwardians over 65 were still in paid work (Thompson 1992: 282).

One similarity you may have noticed is the strong cultural push towards older people remaining independent, with a reluctance simply to move into the homes of their adult children. There is also a major issue to do with poverty; in some ways this is similar to today, when a lack of occupational pensions for many means that older people rely on state benefits, and these are substantially lower than average earnings. In one key respect, however, there is a major difference in that older people are described as 'paupers' and there is the ever-looming threat of the workhouse. There is certainly no mention of support services such as social work. There couldn't be since these simply did not exist. There were no statutory social services at all, and although there were a few social workers, social workers would work for charitable organisations, many of these concerning themselves with the welfare of children.

Optional further study

If you are interested in learning further about the history and background to social work have a look at:

Payne, M. (2005) *The Origins of Social Work: Continuity and Change.* Basingstoke: Palgrave. Chapter 2 covers the period under discussion here.

Powell, F. (2001) *The Politics of Social Work.* London: Sage. Chapter 2.

There can be no doubt that the workhouse was perceived as a major threat in people's lives, constantly reinforcing that they should take responsibility for their own well-being, and not become a burden on the state. The workhouse was the only organisation

---

financed by the state, through Poor Law Guardians appointed to oversee the workhouse in each locality, and this would accommodate people who were unable to care for themselves. Organisations such as residential care homes, daycare establishments and the like were unheard of during this time, although there were some much larger institutions catering for people in specific categories (we will come to this point later).

The question social policy asks is: why? Why such limited state intervention, even when people clearly were in need, and why such a harsh regime?

To answer this we need to introduce you to an important concept in politics and economics: liberalism. This has exerted a strong influence on government policy, justifying lack of activity rather than state intervention.

Key idea 2.1: **Liberalism**

Adam Smith was an eighteenth-century thinker now best known for his economic views and above all his belief in the 'free' market. His most well-known work was *An Inquiry Into the Nature and Causes of the Wealth of Nations*, published in 1776. By the market he means what we would now call a capitalist free market, and 'free market forces'. What this means is that anyone has the right to enter a market; capital is required to start a business and once established each person in a market is able to negotiate whatever deals they like on whatever terms they choose. Meeting consumer needs will, Adam Smith argues, bring the reward of prosperity, by providing:

- what consumers want;
- what consumers are able to pay for – 'effective demand';
- what consumers are willing to pay you for (i.e. your prices are competitive, since your fellow suppliers are all able and entitled to compete against you for price).

Similarly, those who choose not to be suppliers in the market can choose instead to sell their labour to employers, but here again the price of labour is determined by the operation of free market forces. So labourers compete with each other for work, and so in a sense force wages down; but also employers compete for employees and this may force wages up. This is what Adam Smith called 'enlightened self-interest'.

There are a number of implications with this, but for the time being it is worth simply noting the most significant assumptions, namely:

- interference with the market is wrong and always to be avoided;
- since opportunities are open to all, there is no reason why some people should be exempt and exclude themselves from the market by, for example, relying on other people's charity – indeed by doing so they distort the market, so this has to be prevented, and a very clear message given to people that they are responsible for their own well-being, and should not expect help from others.

In its purest form, this means that the state should have no role whatsoever, other than to regulate the market to ensure that it is truly 'free'. However, in reality few governments or states could do this, since it would then result in people literally starving to death. Instead the state does adopt a minimal role to help those on the brink of absolute poverty – at risk of starvation – but does so in a way which stigmatises people to ensure that others do not look on with jealousy or envy and feel there is a 'soft option'. In this sense the role of the state becomes 'residual'.

You may have noticed that these explanations include a number of words that may be new to you. It would be a good idea to keep a separate list of words in a kind of glossary so that you become confident in writing about social policy.

If you accept Adam Smith's theory and its implications, then you may begin to understand how workhouses came to exist and why during the Edwardian period the workhouse was the only institution run by the state to which people could turn if they were destitute. For Smith's ideas had a strong influence on government policy right through the nineteenth century, beginning with the change in the Poor Law instituted through the 1834 Poor Law Amendment Act, which introduced workhouses into major towns and villages.

Clearly enshrined in these ideas is that the poor were responsible for their own poverty, and it is not surprising that the workhouse was as forbidding and as threatening as Lansbury describes it in our case study, for it was intended to be unwelcoming and punitive, a place of last resort, a place to be genuinely feared. Workhouse people were ostracised and heavily stigmatised (if you know Dickens's *Oliver Twist* you may recall that the undertaker's apprentice, Noah Claypole, insults Oliver by calling him 'workhouse' as a name because as an orphan he was brought up in one). They were often called 'paupers' as opposed to being 'the poor', a point we shall pick up later.

It was in theory possible to be released from the workhouse, since no one was compelled to enter it, but in practice this was well-nigh impossible since workhouse inmates could not earn money to enable them to secure employment in the open market. Consequently it's no surprise that for many older people entry to the workhouse was the last place of residence and many actually died there.

At the start of the twenty-first century this policy may sound as though it is verging on the barbaric. However, it is important to recognise that the economic theory that

---

underpinned liberalism included some attractive political principles and implications. These are that it answered certain key questions that we should all ask about the relationship between individual and the state.

Table 2.1: Liberalism's answers to some key questions

Question	Answer
To what extent should people be free from state interference in their lives?	As free as possible (this is essentially why this approach is known as liberalism)
Why then should people obey the state?	Because it is in their interests to do so since the state establishes certain ground rules and protects people
To whom are we responsible?	To ourselves
What can we expect from the state?	A promise not intervene in our everyday lives, minimal state intervention, help only in the most extreme circumstances
Can people help each other?	Of course if they want to, they are free to do so, but there is no duty or obligation
When is it legitimate for the state to intervene in people's lives?	Only in the defence of national interests, to protect people from abusing each other, to maintain law and order

Returning to our case study, it is now clear how the lived experience of older people in the Edwardian era reflected many liberalist ideas. This does not just centre on the existence of the workhouse, but is reflected in the complete lack of support services or any mention of the role of social work. Indeed a strictly liberalist view of social work would say that social work can only exist as an activity if people are prepared to pay for the services of social workers, or else if social workers are needed to maintain law and order. Thus by the time of our case study, one key area of social work that had begun to be developed was that of the probation service, set up to assist the courts to maintain law and order through the supervision of offenders – either instead of, or after, a custodial sentence. This form of social work, which originated in missionary work in the London police courts, was put onto a statutory footing by the Probation of Offenders Act 1907 together with the establishment of borstals for young offenders.

At this point we need to highlight one other point in our case study – pauperism. Why was this phrase used rather than poverty? In short, because paupers were individuals whereas poverty is a social construct, it is a feature of the economy, something outside of people. Because of the particular interpretation of economic theory at the time – deriving from Adam Smith, quite often referred to as 'classical economic theories' – and the predomination of liberalist ideas, the emphasis is very much on paupers and pauperism. People were held to be accountable and responsible for their own poverty, which of course carries the assumption that people do not work because they choose not to, rather than because they cannot do so or because they have few skills and cannot command a large wage or salary. For the moment we do not need to go into the detail of how economics works, but we do need to examine some other ideas that reinforced the notion that poverty is a personal issue, not a social or economic matter.

> If this section has inspired you to learn more about liberalism, there is a much more comprehensive summary of the origins of liberalism and its various forms in Chapter 1 of O'Brien and Penna (1998) *Theorising Welfare*.

Key idea 2.2: **Social Darwinism**

The term 'pauperism' is interesting in that it conveys the full flavour of what is sometimes referred to as social Darwinism. Derived and adapted from Darwin's notion of evolution, natural selection and the hierarchy of species, social Darwinism equates people's wealth and well-being to their contribution to society and their superiority. In other words, the fittest and most superior do best. Hence it would only be natural for those with power and superiority to encourage the fittest to pursue their own interests, and not to be too concerned about the condition of others, who are less fit, less able, and – in effect – lesser human beings. Thus poverty becomes conceptualised as a disease: 'congenital idleness'.

It is easy to see how this can lead to a belief in natural superiority that must promote itself, and therefore can take advantage of the weaker, the inferior. Such ideas can justify expansion of the British Empire, colonialism, through belief in racial superiority, as well as the establishment of institutions for the less able (often also called colonies) through a belief in physical or mental superiority. They can also justify the power of men to control the lives of women, the assumption being that men are stronger and therefore more able and fitter. Such ideas, taken to an extreme eugenicist form, justify attempts to control, or in extreme cases to remove, those in society who are deemed to be 'defective' in some way. Hence serious attempts to prevent people with learning disabilities having children took place shortly after the Edwardian period when Parliament debated compulsory sterilisation (in the debate leading up to the Mental Deficiency Act 1913). Globally, eugenicist ideas have had a major catastrophic effect in justifying wide-scale genocide – the events of the Holocaust being the obvious example, although not unique.

> If you want to know more about this last point, have a look at Chapter 2 of Williams (2009) *Social Work with People with Learning Difficulties*.

Poverty was therefore not seen as a social issue or social concern, but rather as a demonstration that there was a need to control the poor to stop the spread of the 'disease' of pauperism, and to prevent the proliferation of poor people. Or, to put it crudely, to stop them breeding. Thus when workhouses were originally introduced, men were separated from women even if they were married, and in all institutions created during the Victoria era (for example asylums, institutions for people with learning disabilities, children's homes) the sexes were strictly segregated (Williams 1989).

There is a clear connection here with our next the idea: scientific rationalism.

Key idea 2.3: **Scientific rationalism and institutions**

A systematic approach to the classification of human beings ran alongside the concern with the consequences of industrialisation in the nineteenth century and the need to sustain and develop a population who were 'fit' for work. This meant that, although policymakers were committed to principles of liberalism, they were also keen to design and build institutions that reinforced social control measures. The workhouses were complemented by a whole range of institutions determined to segregate those deemed to be a problem in society: for example, the mentally ill, the learning disabled, and lawbreakers. Significantly these groups were not referred to by these terms. In this area of scientific classification and stigmatisation, these groups were more usually referred to as 'lunatics', 'defectives' and 'criminals'. To show how this links with social Darwinism read the following extract.

By the end of the nineteenth century, both the state and voluntary organizations had constructed a complex array of institutions designed to house, care for or reform a variety of people who were seen as constituting different types of social problem: the workhouse, the prison, the asylum, the school, borstals and reformatories, hospitals, and residential institutions for children. Each institution had its own particular character but all shared some common features. They all invoked the need to segregate the 'problem' – to subject it to an institutional regime separated from the rest of society. They all laid claim to a potential for reform – to remake the problem into a person capable, as the Prison Department put it, of 'leading a good and useful life'. And, in the service of reform, they all increasingly laid claim to a specialist or expert 'knowledge-base' – a set of scientifically based understandings of the problem and the principles of reform. These were intended to be productive institutions, taking in flawed human material, working on it in accordance with scientific principles and through such work creating a product useful to society ...

Hand in hand with the reconstruction and development of institutions went an enormous growth of the scientific classification and examination of the human population. Based on medical, biological and subsequently psychological sciences, there was a feverish endeavour to divide, sub-divide, analyse and categorize different groups within the population ... We can indicate some of the major classificatory principles. One was the principle of age – the identification and conceptualization of childhood and the establishment of the principles of 'normal childhood development'; followed by the increasingly significant demarcation of adolescence as a distinct phase of life to be separated from both childhood and adulthood; and finally, the discovery and segregation of old age as a further distinct stage characterized by dependency.

Clarke (1993) *Crisis in Care? Challenges to Social Work*: 6–7

Social policy and older people in the Edwardian period

So how did all the ideas described in this chapter come together to explain the position of older people in the Edwardian period?

Critical thinking exercise 2.2

Taking each of the ideas we have looked at so far – liberalism, social Darwinism and scientific rationalism – explain how each of them helps us to understand the position of older people described in the case study.

You may have found this exercise quite challenging because the connections are not absolutely obvious and immediate. However, if you think about it, liberalist ideas certainly explain why there appears to be a complete absence of state intervention in supporting and promoting the welfare of older people. Everything is left to the family. This chimes totally with liberalist ideas that people should be as free as possible from state intervention, that people are responsible for looking after themselves, and it is fairly clear why this notion of individual responsibility extends at least as far as other immediate members of the family (but usually no further). So in the case study the emphasis is very much on individual experience, and the consequences of growing old are very much individual consequences. For a small elite there were pensions, but for the vast majority of ordinary working people there were none. In the early Edwardian period there were certainly no state pensions, but things did begin to change, as we shall see in the next section. It must be now quite clear to you how the economic principle of free market forces left many older people working right until the very end of their lives, and clearly it was accepted that this is what people should generally do.

It is also clear from the case study how much people feared the workhouse, and how frightening and threatening such institutions would be. Workhouses were part of the system of classification and certainly part of the state control mechanism: the poor were a threat to society, even if they were old and unable to care for themselves. They were also implicated in the belief that the poor were somehow inferior, so older people in Edwardian times would have been absolutely desperate to avoid the workhouse at all costs, not just because it was unpleasant, but because they themselves would be labelled as paupers, and therefore seen to be inferior. This in turn would have reflected on their families, even though it might have been totally unreasonable to expect many families to be able to provide financial support for their aged relatives.

What changed and why?

The Edwardian period marks a turning point in social policy since during this decade, 1901–1910, a number of social policy initiatives were introduced that had a dramatic impact on the improvement of the health and well-being of many people, not just the older population. Some of these were motivated simply by concern about the state of the nation, particular the physical state of young people, as result of the lack of fit recruits for the Boer War in the 1890s (Williams 1989: 155). This was a clear reflection of concerns about physical degeneracy, race, nationhood and all the other ideas that have been mentioned already. At the same time, however, there was a realisation that the plight of many older people should be addressed simply on humanitarian grounds, although some commentators would argue that this was considerably influenced by the development of social and political pressure (Digby 1989; Midwinter 1994). Morally it was recognised that it was not right simply to adopt a punitive approach to people who could not carry on working due to frailty or disability connected to their age.

To this we might add, although this is conjectural, the influence of the first social scientific surveys of poverty. The Rowntree survey of poverty in York carried out in 1901 has already been mentioned in the case study. Preceding this was a systematic survey of poverty carried out by Booth (*The Bitter Cry of Outcast London*, 1883; *In Darkest England and the Way Out*, 1890), who estimated that 30 per cent of the population of London were living in poverty. So now there is a basis for real knowledge about the extent of poverty and therefore potentially grounds for a change in public attitude. The clash between those who believed the state should intervene in poverty and those who were still firmly wedded to pure liberalist ideas was played out in the debates in the Royal Commission on the Reform of the Poor Laws, 1905–1909, which resulted in an influential minority report written by Sidney and Beatrice Webb.

For older people the policy initiative which had the greatest impact was the introduction of state pensions during the Edwardian period, implemented by the Old Age Pensions Act 1908. Although these were means-tested, it did prevent people aged 70 or above having to seek refuge in the workhouse, and paved the way for a pension system based on the insurance principle, following on from the passing of the first national insurance legislation in 1911. In a sense the limitations of the scheme were not so important as the beginnings of the break with liberalism, and the symbolic move towards more state support for older people, which supplanted punitive measures.

However, although there was a welter of small-scale measures in this period, successive governments remained firmly committed to liberalist principles generally. Throughout the

1920s and 1930s there were few social reforms quite on the scale that occurred between 1906 and 1911. The major change occurred in the period just after the Second World War, which is the subject of the next chapter. In the meantime we need to consider the extent to which the kinds of ideas explored in this chapter have influenced contemporary social policy and social work practice with older people.

Liberalism, its influences and social work with older people

Liberalism, as we have seen, is firmly connected to classical economic theory. Both have contemporary equivalents. For liberalism is the precursor or forerunner of the New Right policies which dominated government in the 1980s in Britain, while updated classical economic theory which ran alongside them is monetarism. In the next exercise you are asked to identify the elements of thinking and policy described in this chapter that may still have influences today, paying particular attention to the implications for older people.

In order to carry out this exercise you will need to focus on four particular areas. The first is freedom. Liberalists are keen defenders of freedom, arguing that in order for people to be free they must be free of state interference and state intervention in their lives. People should be left alone. This is quite often described as 'negative freedom', meaning that it is freedom from intervention. The opposite is 'positive freedom', which argues that people are only free in any meaningful sense if they have certain basic needs met and thereby can participate fully in society. However, that is not what liberalists understand by freedom since a consequence of trying to ensure that everyone is equally able to participate is that there are unjustifiable controls over people through a strong regulatory framework which would inevitably include high taxation.

The second, related, area is the free market. Freedom to buy and sell goods at whatever price can be negotiated between the buyer and seller is a fundamental principle of the free market economy. Its great advantage is that it does not require a system of regulation of the prices themselves, since market forces will determine these. Free market forces also regulate supply and demand, so that if goods are abundant then the price drops and more consumers are able to buy them, whereas in time of scarcity prices rise and so few people can afford the goods. There is no need for the government to make rules about who has what since the law of supply and demand, as it is called, will sort this out. What applies to the purchase and sale of goods applies equally to the purchase and sale of labour so that shortages of skills will mean that wages or salaries rise, whereas too many people chasing too few jobs results in wages falling and some people becoming unemployed, and then having to seek lower-paid employment.

It follows from all this that individuals have to take responsibility for themselves, and liberalists are very keen to assert the importance of individual responsibility, individual decision-making, and individuals being the best people to decide what they need. People do not have obligations to wider society, although clearly family members do have obligations to each other, and people have no need to concern themselves about relative levels of wealth or poverty. However, there is nothing to stop people voluntarily giving up their income through contributions to charity or through some other means of sharing responsibility. Updating this, one might say that people are perfectly at liberty to arrange services for themselves, sometimes paid, sometimes voluntary, and this is the ideal. Hence updated liberalism, or neo-liberalism (meaning simply new liberalism), asserts the importance of freedom of choice, and the ability to choose how to further one's own interests.

The consequence of all of this for government is that its role is clearly circumscribed. It must set out a strong system of law and order for ensuring that basic freedoms are respected. The most fundamental of these is the right not to be subject to arbitrary assaults by another country or another individual. The basic system for operating businesses must be established and maintained, but the government does not have to concern itself with issues of social justice since to do so would effectively lead to deprivation of people of money which they had legitimately earned in the open market and this would be a severe curtailment of personal freedom.

What impact do you think these ideas have today, and specifically what impact do you think they would have on social work with older people?

Critical thinking exercise 2.3

In the left-hand column of Table 2.2 you will find some of the key ideas that we have discussed in this chapter. In the right-hand column write down some ideas about specific examples in relation to social work practice and older people.

Table 2.2

Key ideas	Influences on current policy: social work practice and older people examples
Freedom (freedom from state interference, individual freedom)	
Free market forces (prices regulate markets, the law of supply and demand)	
Individualism (individual responsibility and accountability)	
Role of government (residual but strong on defence and law and order)	

You will find some suggestions as to points you might have raised in the exercise answers at the back of this book.

If you found this exercise very difficult, you may want to look at it again after you've looked at Chapter 4, which explores the changes in welfare provision that occurred in the 1980s and early 1990s, the most important of which is the introduction of care management implemented through the National Health Service and Community Care Act 1990.

Postscript

Returning to the case study, you may have had a mixture of feelings about the experiences of older people 100 years ago, but one aspect that may not be immediately obvious is that in some ways older people were better off. At the end of the detailed sociological investigation, based on people talking about their own experiences, the authors of the study came to this conclusion.

Demographic change has transformed the position of the old in the 20th century perhaps more than any other group in the family. The old are now treble the proportion of the British population than they were in the 1900s. They live much longer, but in relative terms they are even poorer. As a proportion of average adult earnings, modern state pensions are less than those of Lloyd George [the pensions introduced by the 1908 Act] ... Worse still even if fit they have usually been compelled to retire from their jobs ... Four out of 10 of those over 65 now live alone: in Edwardian times it was only one ... And a small minority are still forced to wait for death sitting listlessly around the walls of former general wards of (renamed) workhouses, successors of Edwardian paupers.

Thompson (1992) *The Edwardians* : 282.3

You may well consider the last point overstated, but it is certainly food for thought.

Chapter Summary

In this chapter you were presented with a case study of the experience of older people in the Edwardian era in Britain, 1901 to 1910. This included a graphic description of a visit to the workhouse. You were then asked to think about the contrast between the situation described in the case study and Britain today.

The chapter then summarised three key ideas that would have exerted considerable influence on the lived experience of older people during the Edwardian era. The first perspective, which has both an economic and political dimension, was liberalism. You now know that this is a specific approach to policy, and you must remember to be careful not to confuse it with the word 'liberal' or the names of political parties such as the Liberal Democrats. The second idea, strongly influential in some quarters in the first part of the twentieth century, was social Darwinism. This is closely associated with eugenics, which incorporates a belief in racial and gender superiority, as well as justifying harsh segregation of the poor, who become perceived as inferior or lesser human beings. The third set of ideas is scientific rationalism, which in social work terms led to a very firm belief in the power of segregated institutions to promote the well-being of specific groups.

You were then invited to think about how all of these ideas help explain the lived experience of older people during the Edwardian era. This was followed by a brief summary of policy changes that occurred during this time, chief of which was the introduction of old age pensions 100 years ago in 1908. Finally you were asked to consider how traces of these ideas may still be found in contemporary social policy.

In the next chapter we move on to consider the dramatic changes that came about with the creation the welfare state. As in this chapter we will analyse a case study by exploring some of the ideas that came to the fore at the time, particularly social democratic ideas and the move towards Keynesian interventionist economic policies. This will include a different interpretation of freedom, introducing notions of citizenship, and laying the foundations for the development of a compartmentalised social work service, divided according to service user group.

Further reading

History of social work

Payne, M. (2005) *The Origins of Social Work: Continuity and Change.* Basingstoke: Palgrave.

Excellent over-view of social work history. Chapter 2 covers the period under discussion here.

Clarke, J. (1993) *A Crisis in Care? Challenges to Social Work.* London: Sage.

Strong on analysis and explanation of policy shifts that have influenced the history of social work, especially more recent developments.

Powell, F. (2001) *The Politics of Social Work.* London: Sage.

Puts social work in a broader political context. Chapter 2 is particularly relevant to the material covered in this chapter.

Background to developments in social policy

Digby, A. (1989) *British Welfare Policy: Workhouse To Workfare.* London: Faber and Faber.

A concise, readable summary of the major developments in social policy during the twentieth century.

Midwinter, E. (1994) *The Development of Social Welfare In Britain.* Buckingham: Open University Press.

A good alternative to Digby, more narrative in its approach, but with more detail.

Bochel, H., Bochel, C., Page, R. and Sykes, R. (2009) *Social Policy: Issues and Developments* (2nd edition). London: Pearson.
A sound, comprehensive basic text in social policy. Covers all key social policy areas.

Lavalette, M. and Pratt, A. (2005) *Social Policy: Theories, Concepts and Issues.* London: Sage.
A good social policy textbook for students who need a more challenging introduction to social policy. An excellent introduction to theory and strongly recommended.

O'Brien, M. and Penna, S. (1998) *Theorising Welfare.* London: Sage.
A really stimulating and challenging textbook for students who are confident in dealing with theories. Recommended particularly for students for final year of social policy degree or studying for Masters.

Williams, F. (1989) *Social Policy: A Critical Introduction.* Cambridge: Polity Press.
Although now dated, one of the best introductions to a feminist social policy perspective.

3

The Creation of the Welfare State: **The End of the Poor Law and a New Beginning**

Robert Johns

Achieving a Social Work or Social Policy Degree

Exercises in this chapter will focus on

⊙ skill 3   relating different views to underlying philosophies or ideologies
⊙ skill 4   evaluating different perspectives and ideas

The chapter is relevant to a number of Social Policy Benchmarks.

3.2   origins and development of UK welfare institutions and the social and
        demographic contexts in which they have operated
        main features of the interrelationship between social policies and
        differently placed communities, families and individuals
3.3   key concepts and theories of welfare
        theories of the state and policymaking
        history of contemporary social problems and of social policy responses
        to them

Its content is also of particular relevance to the following Social Work Subject
Benchmarks.

5.1.2 the location of contemporary social work within historical, comparative and
        global perspectives
        the changing demography and cultures of communities
        the complex relationships between public, social and political philosophies,
        policies and priorities and the organisation and practice of social work

Introduction

When people mention the 'welfare', they sometimes appear to be talking about the
benefit system, but are occasionally referring to the role of social workers. Occasionally
they get the two mixed up and do not distinguish between them at all. To some extent
this is understandable. In many people's minds social work is associated with the
welfare state – comprehensive government intervention intended to improve people's
well-being: financial, educational, physical and social. Social work is clearly aimed at the
social, but it is not surprising that people see the whole welfare state as a package and

automatically make certain kinds of connections, so linking social care and well-being with state benefits that help people avoid poverty is logical. This logic is confirmed by history, for many of the developments that comprise the welfare state – the National Health Service, the social security and benefit system, the development of secondary education, and the establishment of social work as primarily a local authority service – occurred during a comparatively short period, 1946–1948.

This chapter focuses on that period, connecting the immediate post-war developments in the welfare state to fundamental changes in social policy thinking which, in turn, connect to changing ideas about the economy and about people's role in society. This chapter will ask you to develop some skills in connecting social policy initiatives to underlying theories or ideas. In doing so you will need to compare the differences between social policy thinking in this period and the prevailing ideology of the Edwardian period covered in Chapter 2. Comparing and evaluating theories, and connecting these to policy outcomes, is clearly an important skill which you will be able to develop both in this chapter and in Chapter 4.

CASE STUDY

The day the welfare state began

The following is an extract quoted in Never Again, *a detailed political history of the 1945–1951 period.*

> I can remember this particular day. Everything was in a radius of a few minutes' walk, and she [mother] went to the opticians. Obviously she'd got the prescription from the doctor. She went and she got tested for new glasses. Then she went further down the road ... for the chiropodist. She had her feet done. Then she went back to the doctor's because she'd been having trouble with her ears and the doctor said ... he would fix her up with a hearing aid. And I remember – me mother was a very funny woman – I remember her saying to the doctor on the way out, 'Well, the undertaker's is on the way home. Everything's going on, I might as well call in there on the way home!'

quoted in **Hennessy** (1992: 174)

In the above extract, Alice Law was talking about her mother's experience on the first day when the welfare state was officially inaugurated in Britain, 5th July 1948. Although a number of other aspects of the welfare state had already been instituted, the chief component of what most people call the welfare state, the National Health Service, was officially brought into being on that day. As can be seen from the quotation, its coverage was truly wide-ranging: general medical care, eyes, hearing, chiropody, and – although Alice's mother didn't manage to fit this into her busy schedule – dentistry.

Critical thinking exercise 3.1

Compare this experience with the experience of older people in Edwardian times you read about in Chapter 1.

What are the key differences? What do you think has changed?

In some ways the differences could not be more stark. We seemed to have moved from pauperism and the threat of the workhouse to a system of entitlement, and generous entitlement at that. We now have a picture of an older woman confidently revelling in the new provisions of the welfare state, rather like someone who has won the lottery. She is enthusiastically exercising her right to free provision across the widest range of healthcare.

In social policy terms we have moved away from a 'residual' approach whereby only people in the direst of circumstances would be offered assistance, to one where everyone is entitled to services on the basis of need. There is no hint of a mention of financial contributions to services here, and at the time when the welfare state was founded, it was not intended that people should pay for the majority of services. Even prescriptions were originally free to all. You may already be aware that much of the planning behind the introduction of the welfare state can be traced to the Beveridge Report of 1942, officially entitled the *Social Insurance and Allied Services Report*, which identified 'five giants', as Beveridge called them: illness, ignorance, disease, squalor, and want.

Table 3.1 summarises the social policy responses to that Report.

Table 3.1

Social evil or challenge: Beveridge's 'giant'	Welfare state-related proposal	Welfare state-related social policy
Illness	Introduce a National Health Service, free for all	National Health Service Act 1946
Disease		
Squalor	Improved housing conditions, public health developments	Rebuilding programmes including development of first New Towns
Ignorance	Free universal secondary education	Education Act 1944
Want	Contributory National Insurance scheme, social security system	National Insurance Act 1946, National Assistance Act 1948, family allowances, unemployment benefit

Underpinning all of this is a fundamental change of philosophy, namely the shift already identified from the residual to entitlement, or from selectivity to universality. In this chapter we will explore why there was this fundamental shift, and also invite you to think about the implications of it since this distinction is very important if you are to be able to analyse social policy developments.

Critical thinking exercise 3.2

At this stage you may find it helpful to draw up a glossary to remind you of the differences in meaning of these terms, as they will keep occurring in social policy texts. For example:

residual – refers to provision for only those who can demonstrate they have absolutely no other means of making provision for themselves;

entitlement – implies some kind of legal right to provision whether or not someone is actually in need of that particular provision.

In a short phrase, summarise in your own words in a way which you will remember the meanings of:

selectivity = ?

universality = ?

Now we need to make a couple of comments about how this related to older people specifically.

As well as the development in relation to healthcare, of critical importance to many older people was the much more generous approach to pensions introduced by the welfare state. Although pensions were first introduced in the Edwardian era, relatively speaking very few people qualified for them, since there were fewer older people in the age group. Demographically the proportion of older people in the Edwardian years was much smaller than it was in the 1940s, and of course much smaller than it is now, but also the entitlement thresholds were higher. The Beveridge Report proposed a system of pensions for all, based on contributions to the National Insurance scheme. However, the level of pension was intended to be reasonably generous, so that eventually when all workers had been able to pay sufficient contributions to the fund, virtually everyone in the country would be entitled to a pension almost equivalent to their previous standard of living, a pension 'earned' through their contributions.

However, this would not apply to everyone. Beveridge proposed special rules for married women.

Critical thinking exercise 3.3

Why do you think these special rules were needed? What assumptions lay behind this? Stop to think about this before reading on, as the answer follows immediately.

Because at that time married women were expected not to work, and indeed in some professions were required to resign if they got married, Beveridge proposed rules that entitled them to pensions on the basis of their husband's contributions to the National Insurance scheme. Note a woman had to be married to be thus entitled: this is an example of social policy reflecting cultural norms, and assumptions about gender roles. If you look at the current rules for entitlement to pensions you will still find the vestiges of this: in certain circumstances a person is allowed to claim a pension through someone else's contributions. That someone else now is not just a husband, but can include a spouse or civil partner, yet the underlying thinking remains and claimants still have to be in a formally recognised legal relationship in order to qualify.

Instead of introducing the scheme exactly as Beveridge proposed, the government of the day brought forward these supposedly more generous rates and allowed people to claim these despite not having notionally yet made contributions to pay for them. To quote from Hennessy (1992) once again:

> In one area, however, Griffiths [Minister of National Insurance] allowed his generous impulses full rein. Beveridge, worried by the increasing proportion of elderly people in the population as a whole (in 1901 6.2% were of pensionable age; by 1942 this had risen to 20.8%), recommended that pensions should be gradually raised to the new rate over twenty years. Griffiths decided to do it in one go as 'The men and women who [in 1946] had already retired had experienced a tough life. In their youth they had been caught by the 1914 war, in middle age they had experienced the indignities of the depression, and in 1940 had stood firm as a rock in the nation's hour of trial.' Within three months of the Act receiving royal assent, a single pensioner was receiving 25 shillings a week (£1.25) and a married couple 42 shillings (£2.10).
>
> **Hennessy** (1992: 131)

As well as offering an insight into the rationale, this extract provides information about another difference: the dramatic increase in proportion of older people in the population.

Critical thinking exercise 3.4

Look at this quotation again and answer the following questions.

How would you set about finding the comparative information on the proportion of older people in the population today, so that you can compare it with the figures quoted for 1901 and 1942?

What ideas seem to lie behind the rationale for treating older people more generously?

What concepts or ideas appear to be distinguishing social policy in this period from social policy in the Edwardian era?

There are number of ways in which you can access demographic data but the most reliable current information will almost undoubtedly be to look at the census data, available through the Office for National Statistics. This is easily accessible online, with useful and accurate data, based on the statutory census held once every ten years, readily available. There are also more comparative and historical data offered to researchers through the Economic and Social Research Council (for website addresses see end of chapter).

Interestingly, the rationale for treating older people more generously appears to relate to their wider role in society, specifically their assumed contributions to the two world wars, and their experience of survival of the decade of economic depression in the 1930s. The underlying assumption here appears to be that older people were to be rewarded for their contributions as loyal citizens. They were patriotic and worthy of respect and the state or country owed them something. We might also note a marked change to a strong defence of the 'rights' of older people, which appears to emanate from a change to some kind of notion of collective responsibility. Putting the two together it was clear that poverty and older people had become a political issue, reflecting a new ideology. This ideology can be summarised concisely as a shared duty to respect and promote people's rights as citizens.

The policy outcome of all of this took the dramatic form of the formal abolition of the Poor Law and the workhouse. The Poor Law Unions which ran the Poor Law system had actually being abolished by the Local Government Act of 1929 with 'poor relief' responsibilities transferred to counties and county boroughs. In 1934 responsibility for assisting the non-insured unemployed was transferred to the Unemployment Assistance Board. The 1945–48 welfare state legislation effectively made the Poor Law redundant, and it was finally officially abolished by section 1 of the National Assistance Act 1948, which starts with the historic legal statement 'The existing poor law shall cease to have effect'.

Clearly an assumption that the state has a responsibility for the income of older people marks a dramatic shift. Instead of emphasising the ever-looming threat of the workhouse, older people can now look forward to a future with income more or less assured, under the aegis of a political culture where the state accepted responsibility for their well-being. You will therefore not be surprised to learn that alongside this came some social work-related developments. A key component of the National Assistance Act 1948, and part of the Act that is still in force even today (in section 21), concerned the provision by local authorities of residential and other accommodation for people in need. Part Three of the Act stipulated that a local authority could, and in some cases must, provide residential accommodation for people aged 18 or above, although in practice the majority of accommodation was provided for people over the age of 65. If someone could not afford the accommodation they needed, the local authority was required to assess a person's ability to pay, and charge rates in accordance with what they were able to afford (section 22, National Assistance Act 1948, still in force in its original formulation). Note the emphasis on the word 'need'.

Finally, note some key words or concepts that now occur which distinguish social policy approaches to older people in this era from the prevailing ethos of the Edwardian era. Here are just some: entitlements, need, collective provision, contributory, rights, citizenship, local authority provision.

Optional further study

Most social policy texts will assist you in learning further about concepts used in social policy. You may in particular want to have a look at:

Alcock, P. (2008) *Social Policy in Britain* (3rd edition). Basingstoke: Palgrave. Especially Chapters 1 and 12.

Baldock, J., Manning, N. and **Vickerstaff, S.** (eds.) (2007) *Social Policy* (3rd edition). Oxford: Oxford University Press.

Drake, R. (2001) *The Principles of Social Policy.* Basingstoke: Palgrave.

Clearly between the Edwardian period and the period that saw the creation of the welfare state major changes had occurred. We now turn to the question why? What shifts had taken place in thinking? What theories or ideas had developed to justify this?

To answer this we need to introduce two important concepts in politics and economics: social democracy and Keynesian economics. These have both exerted a strong influence on government policy, justifying state intervention in contrast to the marked non-interventionist approach you encountered in the previous chapter. As we have seen, older people were major beneficiaries of this change.

Key idea 3.1: **Collective responsibility and state intervention in welfare**

Social democracy incorporates a wide spectrum of ideas and concepts, some of which have already been covered. The major driving force appears to be notions of citizenship, which carries with it the assumption that people deserve to be treated as people of equal value, and therefore there should not be disproportionate and unfair levels of wealth in society. Society should be egalitarian in the sense that there should be as much equality as possible: this does not presuppose everyone should have exactly the same income, but it would certainly argue for people's equal rights to participate in society, and most especially in the political system. So rules that are manifestly unfair ought to be eliminated. There will be a further discussion of notions of equality in Chapter 4, since challenges to egalitarianism were successful in arguing for a different formulation of the welfare state.

However, for now we need to note that there have been a number of thinkers who have developed social democratic ideas, particularly those centring on citizenship. Some of these developments took place after the welfare state was created, influencing its period of dramatic expansion in the 1960s. Yet some of it derived from the Edwardian era.

An example of revolutionary ideas that had emerged even in Edwardian times was the Minority Report for the Royal Commission into the Poor Law [1905–1909] which was largely written by Sidney and Beatrice Webb. These ideas influenced the development of the Fabian movement, led by the Webbs and so Fabianism, as some social policy texts call it, can be equated with social democratic ideas. The Webbs' core belief was that *socialism in Britain was entirely compatible with the institutions of the state and could, and should, be realised through a Parliamentary route. The state … could be harnessed to promote the collective good and act as a neutral umpire between the demands of different interests* (Alcock et al. 2008: 33).

Originally writing in the 1930s (Tawney's book *Equality* was first published in 1931), the fabian Richard Tawney suggested that the existence and approval of inequality were a fundamental affront to human beings. He believed equality to consist of the three basic principles:

- all humans share a common humanity;
- society should be organised in such a way that its members make the best use of their powers and abilities;
- rewards should be linked to social purposes.

The last point suggests that, for example, the right to property should be conditional on the obligation to service. Those who own property have duties to others, obligations that connect to the notion of citizenship. With its inherent drive towards acquisitiveness, capitalism needed to be tempered in order to achieve the aims of a just society. The institutions that a purely capitalist regime creates would not be consistent with promoting the well-being of all people, indeed was socially divisive. At the same time Tawney did not approve of authoritarian regimes, even if they had socialist ideals. For such regimes would be strongly centralised and hold too much power. Instead the authority of the state to govern must derive from consent of the people, and should be focused on promoting citizens as self-reliant beings, who share obligations to each other, yet whose individual differences are always respected.

Writing at about the period when the welfare state was created, T.H. Marshall set out clearly articulated views as to what constituted citizenship. Marshall exerted a great deal of influence on political thinking in the immediate post-war period, with his political views mirroring the economic approach of Keynes. In a very well-known seminal piece of writing, *Citizenship and Social Class and Other Essays* published in 1950, Marshall divided citizenship into three parts: civil, political and social rights.

- Civil rights refers to individual freedoms such as freedom of speech, the right to own property, freedom of thought, religious freedom, freedom of association and the right to justice, including access to information.
- Political rights refers to the ability to engage in political processes, specifically the right to free elections and a secret ballot, in other words rights to participation in democratic political processes.
- Social rights refers to economic welfare and security with the rights to participate in the cultural life of a society and, effectively, to live the life of a civilised human being.

This approach was later encapsulated in the philosophy of American philosopher John Rawls, who in his *A Theory of Justice* published in 1971, argued for the eventual elimination of inequality within the existing political system. The chances of the least well-off should be maximised in order for them to become as free as the most well-off.

We can summarise all of these views by setting out four essential components of citizenship. In order to become a citizen, someone:

- must be a full member of that society;
- must be able to participate in its government;
- must be entitled to the rights that society confers;
- must be prepared to meet their obligations to other people.

Only if all four of these preconditions of citizenship are met, can someone properly be regarded as a citizen.

Partly as a result of some of these influences (and others) social policy thinking throughout the war years was moving inexorably to a much stronger belief in a society in which people participated fully. Politically this had been achieved by the extension of the franchise to women in the period just after the First World War, but there had also been a remarkable shift towards the view that people as citizens had duties towards each other, and one of those was to ensure that everyone was looked after at the time of need. There was, in fact, a collective responsibility for communal and individual well-being.

We can unpack these ideas by looking at the answers this social democratic or citizenship approach offers to the questions we posed in Chapter 2. As you look at this table, note the differences with the answers provided by liberalism outlined in Chapter 2.

Table 3.2: Social democratic answers to some key questions

Question	Answer
To what extent should people be free from state interference in their lives?	As much as possible but people can only be free to participate fully in society if they have certain basic needs met as citizens, and in order to achieve this others may have to accept some constraints
Why should people obey the state?	Because it is in their interests to do so since the state establishes certain ground rules and provides its citizens with basic essential needs
To whom are we responsible?	To each other
What can we expect from the state?	Basic needs met: health, education, protection from poverty, social care for those in need
Can people help each other?	They should, since there is a duty to do so and it is to some extent imposed by such means as redistribution of wealth through taxation
When is it legitimate for the state to intervene in people's lives?	When necessary to ensure everyone's basic needs are met as citizens and in order to reduce inequality

Critical thinking exercise 3.5

You now have two sets of competing answers to the same basic questions, one above and the other in a similar table in Chapter 2.

Put these answers together so that if you were asked a question about the development of social policy in the first part of the twentieth century, you would be able to answer that question analytically rather than just as narrative. In other words, you would be able to say:

whereas in the Edwardian period it was generally believed that freedom meant ...

at the time when the welfare state was created it was generally believed that freedom meant ...

Consequently as far as older people were concerned in the Edwardian period ...

whereas in the late 1940s ...

Try this out for yourself by completing the sentences above.

If it helps think of it as a matrix (table):

whereas in the Edwardian period it was generally believed that freedom meant ...	at the time when the welfare state was created it was generally believed that freedom meant ...
Consequently as far as older people were concerned in the Edwardian period ...	whereas in the late 1940s ...

Can you see how such an approach would be a very effective way of answering the question analytically? This is the kind of skill you need to develop in the later stages of degree level programmes.

Key idea 3.2: **Keynesian economics: State intervention in the economy**

John Maynard Keynes was a twentieth-century economist, whose name is strongly associated with the growth in welfare states just after the Second World War. In *The General Theory of Employment, Interest and Money* published in 1936, Keynes put forward his theory that free market forces, which were the bedrock of classical liberalism (of the type that we saw in Chapter 2), necessarily led to people being underemployed. Keynes suggested that in a free market there were inefficiencies and wastes due to lack of co-ordination, and this resulted, at worst, at a polarisation of rich and poor. Therefore, he argued, it was essential for the state to take direct action through such measures as currency and credit control, and also investments in the public sector which would have the spin-off effect of pump-priming economic investment and development.

This enabled those who were attracted to Keynesian theory to argue persuasively that government responses to some of the challenges it faces should be quite different from the way it would have responded in the Edwardian era. So for example:

- if people are unemployed, instead of reducing wages which would have the effect of reducing demand even further and therefore risking higher unemployment, governments should concentrate on the demand side;
- so instead of waiting – possibly for a long time – for the demand for goods and services to increase, the government should invest in public works so that in at least one sector more people would be employed;
- if there are problems with the economy, one strategy for government would be to control the amount of currency in circulation or else to control the rate at which banks lent;
- if there were people in relative poverty, it would be acceptable to use government funds to provide an income to relieve poverty, not just on humanitarian grounds but also because by increasing people's income, you also increase demand for goods and services and therefore bring more people into employment;

- government action through the taxation system can to some extent redistribute wealth, and this enables more people to purchase goods and services, which again increases employment opportunities for others;
- redistribution of wealth need not just take the form of money, since taxing the wealthy in order to pay for services, which predominantly poorer people need, is also another form of redistribution;
- overall, the economy should comprise a mixture of private and public-sector enterprises, what would now be called a 'mixed economy'.

It should be added in passing that Keynesian ideas were used by a number of governments throughout the world to control the economy and to justify increased public expenditure, and the growth of the welfare state in Britain was mirrored by similar developments in many other countries, particularly the Scandinavian countries, but also throughout most of western Europe as well as elsewhere.

Social policy and older people in the welfare state period

So how did these ideas come together and what would they say about older people in this period?

Critical thinking exercise 3.6

Connect the two sets of ideas we have looked at so far– citizenship (social democracy) and Keynesian economics – and use them to explain how they would apply to the welfare of older people.

Hopefully you found this exercise not quite as challenging as the exercise in Chapter 1, but it has developed your skills further since here we are asking you to connect ideas.

Combining the notion of citizenship (with its strong declaration that in order to be effective citizens people have to have certain basic needs met) with the Keynesian justification for the state to provide for those basic needs, clears the path for increased pensions, basic healthcare free at the point of delivery, and all the other welfare state services which Alice Law's mother relished.

A more complex connection lies between the notion of freedom implied by citizenship and the Keynesian theory, but intrinsic here is the belief that people's freedom can be sustained and promoted through the state providing for people's basic needs and that this can be achieved within the current economic system.

How about other aspects of citizenship? Citizenship appears to assert the dignity and worth of each individual and by moving to a rights- or entitlement-based approach to social welfare it is clear how this would be attained. Likewise the Keynesian preoccupation with countering employment reflects the value of individuals participating in the economy but also, in a curious way, providing higher incomes for retired people contributes to this. For greater purchasing power for older people means an increase in their demand for goods and services and therefore eventually translates into more employment for others (you could also argue that removing older people from the labour market gives employment to younger people but that is a different argument and somewhat contentious).

Finally, citizenship focuses on people's participation in society and clearly the introduction of a comprehensive system of welfare benefits facilitates this. Apart from enabling people to live longer through improved healthcare, offering protection from poverty should enable people to enjoy quality, fulfilled lives instead of focusing on mere survival.

Can we now say something specifically about the family and older people?

Critical thinking exercise 3.7

Look back at Chapter 2 and in particular the discussion about the links between liberalism and the care of older people by their families. Now that you are aware of the key changes in social policy in the late 1940s, what do you think the implications might be for families?

Try to answer this now without reading on, since one response to this question follows immediately.

In the previous chapter it was explained how the prevailing ideas justified a complete absence of state intervention in supporting and promoting the welfare of older people. Everything was left to the family. This reflected ideas that people should be as free as possible from state intervention, that people were responsible for looking after themselves, and this notion of individual responsibility extended to other immediate members of the family. For a small elite there were pensions, but for the vast majority of ordinary working people there were none.

Now we are in a very different situation. Everyone over a certain age is entitled to a pension, and with the aid of the new national assistance system, every older person would be entitled to a certain minimum income, enough to ensure they were independent. No mention of the workhouse anymore, and no hint of being a liability to other family members. Indeed, a valid supposition might be that with the introduction of state welfare services generally, including social work, older people will generally as a consequence be much more independent of their families. The state now provides residential care if necessary, and although there may well be expectations that families would help in the provision of care, there is certainly no longer any kind of stigma attached to it.

Indeed there may be unintended consequences of this, as we shall see in the following chapter. For transferring responsibility from family to state can unwittingly encourage a situation where older people are expected to live independently of their adult children and this can result in them living not just independent lives, but isolated or segregated lives. We shall see that this is particularly an issue when it comes to the provision of residential social care, which can be experienced as a system for 'warehousing' older people, many of whom may become alienated from the rest of society, including their own families. It is not the purpose of this book to prove whether the welfare state had that effect, but it is intended that you can use this example to explore how social policy can have that kind of impact. Nor is it the intention to comment on whether that consequence is desirable or not; that is a qualitative judgement you will need to make for yourself, balancing the obvious benefits to older people from the advent of the welfare state against some of the possible losses. We will return to this in Chapter 4.

What changed and why?

We conclude this analysis of social policy and older people in the immediate post-war period by putting forward some suggestions as to how and why a dramatic change in social policy occurred.

The period 1945–1948 represents a key turning point in social policy since it heralded the introduction of a truly comprehensive welfare state in Britain, with provisions and entitlements that would now seem remarkably generous. However, it would be wrong to suppose that there was a sudden conversion to a different approach to social policy, for in several ways the establishment of the welfare state was the culmination of a number of influences that occurred from the Edwardian period onwards.

Immediately after the Edwardian period occurred the First World War, with its devastating impact on the population (death or injuries to 2.5 million troops in Britain alone), society and politics. Its reverberations were far-reaching. In social policy terms the immediate effect was the 1918 election campaign fought on the ideal of making the land 'fit for heroes' which established the notion that people had the right to make demands on the state and that there was a collective responsibility to provide for people's well-being (Gladstone 1999: 22–23).

From the end of the First World War to the beginning of the second, a number of changes occurred that also help to explain the establishment of the welfare state. In summary these were as follows.

- A reduction in Britain's economic strength, which resulted in losing its leadership position to the growing US economy. Alongside this a loss of political status in the world, and eventually a diminution of the British Empire.
- Loss of economic power was translated into a reduction in manufacturing and contraction of traditional industry (such as coal, shipbuilding, steel and textiles) with the resultant high persistent unemployment and industrial unrest.

The so-called Depression saw the hunger marches with its pleas for the basic right to work in order to be able to earn a living; this was in the context of constantly rising unemployment throughout the 1920s, culminating in a published unemployment rate of 22.1 per cent in 1932 (Hicks and Allen 1999: 24).

- Large-scale local authority-financed house building which included slum clearance and concerted efforts to reduce overcrowding in housing. Allied with this are improvements in healthcare with an increasing proportion of the population working in the public sector. Earlier improvements in public health continued so that it is no longer routine to have mass epidemics of infectious diseases.

- Politically a key change had been the fall of the Liberal Party, to be replaced by the rise of the Labour movement with its strong connections to trade unions and its claim to be representative of the working class. Although the Liberal government had been instrumental in introducing some welfare reforms in the preceding period, there was some scepticism about welfare reforms that simply perpetuated the Poor Law mentality, and the Labour Party represented a move towards a welfare state controlled by the people themselves rather than one imposed by central government in the interests of the wealthy.

> You will find more detail on these developments in a number of standard social policy texts, in particular Alcock et al. (2008: 30–33).

At this point it is worth repeating the exercise we conducted the end of the last chapter and consider the extent to which the kinds of ideas explored in this chapter have influenced contemporary social policy and social work practice with older people.

Citizenship, Keynesian economics and social work with older people

The promotion of the notion of citizenship that underpinned the introduction of the welfare state ran in parallel with the development of Keynesian economic theory. It is debatable whether the welfare state necessarily required both, but this is an instructive example of political ideology joining forces with economic theory to help drive forward some key social welfare reforms. Even more important for our purposes is that they both have contemporary equivalents, mirrored in contemporary debates.

In the last chapter a connection was drawn between liberalism, monetarism and the New Right policies of the 1980s. Social democracy incorporating citizenship ideals has exerted a strong influence on Labour governments in the UK and indeed on many left-of-centre governments and social policy developments throughout Europe. Likewise, belief in government intervention in the economy and substantial investments of public money to 'kick-start' the economy in times of difficulty are policies which are pure Keynesianism – an obvious recent example being the measures taken by the government in 2008 to avoid a deepening recession triggered by a banking crisis.

As regards older people, there are certainly examples that can be offered that connect specific policies in relation to older people with social democratic ideals and Keynesian economic thinking. Let's look at what some of these might be by starting with the concept of citizenship that underpins social democracy.

It needs to be emphasised that in this context we are not talking about citizenship as a legal concept; this preoccupies many contemporary discussions centring on who is entitled to be regarded as a British citizen and inevitably veering into the issue of refugees and asylum seekers. Instead citizenship is used in social policy in its more philosophical, political or theoretical sense. Although it is not often used in this sense, it is clear that citizenship undergirds the whole belief in the welfare state and that generally people do hold some citizenship principles to be very important. Chief among these in social work is the notion of empowerment, the idea that people should be supported and encouraged to speak for themselves, pursue what matters for them as individuals, claim their rights as independent human beings, simply because they are people, or to be more precise because they are citizens. It is the political notion of citizenship that sets out what these basic rights might be and why: they are inalienable rights, deriving from principle, not dependent on the grace and favour of some autocratic ruler or some political elite.

Allied with this view of rights is a view of freedom that is different from that which liberalists promoted. As we saw in the last chapter, liberalists claim to be keen defenders of freedom, arguing for freedom from state interference and state intervention. This is quite often described as negative freedom, meaning that it is freedom from interference in one's life. Yet that is not what this chapter has been about. For this chapter has been dominated by talk of entitlements, rights to an income, to health and well-being, reflecting a positive view of freedom which argues that people are only free in any meaningful sense if they have certain basic needs met and thereby can participate fully in society, a notion generally attributed to the philosopher T.H. Green. This was certainly the approach adopted by the Labour Party when it won the 1945 general election and its influence has persisted right through to today.

Some examples of a citizenship approach to social policy for older people would include:

- entitlement to an agreed minimum pension for everyone over a certain age;
- a basic income that covers all essential needs;
- entitlement to healthcare regardless of means;
- entitlement to social care regardless of means;
- the right to live independently and to be supported to do so;
- the right to work if an older person wishes to;
- additional financial entitlements for older people with specific needs, such as a disability;
- the right to decide how care is to be provided, regardless of cost.

Closer examination of the list indicates that some of these came into effect with the implementation of the welfare state reforms, and some – not necessarily the same ones – are features of contemporary social policy. Some, of course are aspirations, and not actual policy. For example, older people cannot choose any form of care regardless of cost, since they must convince the local authority that they are in 'need' (section 47 National Health Service and Community Care Act 1990) and then the care is provided in accordance with local authority policies, which inevitably include reference to cost. Similarly in Britain older people do not receive a state pension set at a level where they can live without other means; it is true that if they cannot meet their own needs they can apply for social security or housing supplements but these are means-tested and as soon as means tests are involved the support becomes discretionary and no longer a citizenship entitlement.

Now to Keynesian influences. We saw in the last chapter that the freedom to buy and sell goods at whatever price can be negotiated between the buyer and seller is a fundamental principle of the free market economy in which liberalists believed. Relating this to employment meant no protection from unemployment and consequently a heavy insistence on people taking responsibility for themselves, with all that that implies. Conversely, Keynesianism sees unemployment itself as essentially problematic, indicating slack in the economy, with a need for state intervention, necessary to prevent a ripple effect of other people being unemployed due to a drop in demand for goods and services (inevitable as those who are unemployed have less disposable income and therefore less 'effective' demand for goods and services). Furthermore, in a bid to increase demand for goods and services, a Keynesian would argue for an increase in the state sector itself since increased government spending of itself raises demand for goods and services and therefore provides employment. It also, of course, provides employment directly for public service workers.

So providing generous pensions for older people will increase their ability to buy goods and services and increasing the state care sector for older people both increases employment opportunities for care workers and requires other people to work to maintain the care system: buildings have to be built and maintained, transport is needed, administration is required, and so on.

It may be worth pointing to some potential conflicts of ideals here. In the list above of examples of a citizenship approach to social policy was included the right to work if an older person wishes. This presents a dilemma since although a 70-year-old in active employment presumably has greater spending power than someone of the same age who is retired, it may also be the case that they block employment opportunities for younger people and that would mitigate against the Keynesian ideal of increasing the number of people in employment. This is worth mentioning as it may explain an apparent inconsistency in people's rights: people generally have the right to work but employers have a right to insist that people over a certain age retire. In other words, the absolute right to employment does not apply to older people – an interesting apparent anomaly, and one which you may want to think about as it does raise the issue of how to decide between competing rights and entitlements, how to determine whose rights ultimately count. Reconciling competing claims is an essential feature of social policy.

So now, taking these two key ideas – citizenship and belief in government intervention in the economy – what influence do you think they have exerted on social policy and social work practice in relation to older people?

Critical thinking exercise 3.8

In the left-hand column of Table 3.3 you'll find some of the key ideas discussed in this chapter. In the right-hand column write down some ideas about specific examples in relation to social work practice and older people. Once you have finished you will be able to compare your answers with the exercise completed at the end of Chapter 2.

Table 3.3

Key ideas	Influences on current policy: Social work practice and older people examples
Positive freedom: freedom to participate fully in society	
Mixed economy: state sector, private and independent sector	
Collectivism: people are responsible for each other	
Role of government as major provider of welfare	

You will find some suggestions as to points you might have raised in the exercise answers at the back of this book.

Postscript

The advent of the welfare state may appear, at first sight, to have been an unqualified boon for older people but not everyone was enthusiastic. We have already seen in Chapter 2 that liberalists would be bound to assert the importance of individual responsibility and also argue that the cost of ensuring that everyone is equally able to participate in society is too high (see section in Chapter 2 headed 'Liberalism, its influences and social work with older people' for this argument). An unintended consequence, some argued, was the transfer of responsibility from the individual to the state. If people could rely on the state to support them in all circumstances, what incentive lay in people looking after their own interests? What about relatives and family responsibility for caring for older people which the Edwardians took for granted?

 The great fear was that the wider availability of domiciliary care would be used by carers to abandon elderly relatives to the state.

Means (1995)

Thus social work did not develop as rapidly as other areas of the welfare state and came under intense scrutiny in the period to be studied in the next chapter, the 1980s.

Chapter Summary

In this chapter you were presented with a case study of the experience of an older person heralding the arrival of the welfare state in Britain in 1948. This involved a dramatic change away from Edwardian policy towards a comprehensive government-run system in which people were entitled to have basic needs met. For older people the policy initiative which had the greatest impact at the time was the formal abolition of the Poor Law, and all that that represented.

The chapter offered some reasons for this dramatic change, including reference to the highly influential Beveridge Report. More broadly, welfare state developments were located within two key sets of ideas. The first was the social democratic notion of entitlement based on citizenship rights, a philosophical position that resulted in political action and helps to explain much of contemporary social policy. The second relates to the economic theory of Keynes with its core commitment to state intervention in the economy which represents a sharp turn away form the previous non-interventionist approaches of monetarism and liberalism.

We then considered the links between these sets of ideas and social policy regarding older people. The list offered has significant similarities with the rights and entitlements of older people today yet there are some limitations and examples of current social policy that do not quite accord with the theoretical views considered earlier in the chapter. This led to a final consideration of connections between ideas considered in this chapter and contemporary social policy.

In the next chapter we move on to consider the challenges encountered by the welfare state in the 1980s during a period of economic difficulty and retrenchment. Here we will see played out a conflict between the theories and ideals summarised in Chapters 2 and 3: a resurgence of liberalism clashing with welfare state ideals and principles. This led to a reformulation of social policy particularly in relation to older people, with an attempt to relocate responsibility for older people's welfare away from the state and more towards themselves and their families.

Further reading

Alcock, P. (2008) *Social Policy in Britain* (3rd edition). Basingstoke: Palgrave.
Excellent basic social policy text. Chapters 1 and 12 especially relevant to this chapter.
Baldock, J., Manning, N. and Vickerstaff, S. (eds.) (2007) *Social Policy* (3rd edition). Oxford University Press.
An alternative recommended basic social policy text.
Drake, R. (2001) *The Principles of Social Policy*. Basingstoke: Palgrave.
One of the few texts that focuses on values and principles that underpin social policy.
Gladstone, D. (1999) *The Twentieth Century Welfare State*. Basingstoke: Palgrave.
Clear, readable introduction to social policy developments in the period covered in this chapter.
Hicks, J. and Allen, G. (1999) *A Century of Change: Trends in UK Statistics since 1900*. London: House of Commons.
For students particularly interested in statistical information relevant to this period.
Payne M. (2005) *The Origins of Social Work: Continuity and Change*. Basingstoke: Palgrave.
Covers this period well.

Websites
Office for National Statistics: **www.ons.gov.uk**
ESRC Census Programme: **census.ac.uk**
Both websites provide a wealth of dependable statistical data. Great for assignments.

4

From State Welfare to a Mixed Economy:
The Era of Community Care

Robert Johns

Achieving a Social Work or Social Policy Degree

Exercises in this chapter will focus on

- ⊙ skill 1   demonstrating understanding and application of theoretical ideas
- ⊙ skill 3   relating different views to underlying philosophies or ideologies
- ⊙ skill 4   evaluating different perspectives and ideas

As with Chapter 3, it is relevant to the following Social Policy Benchmarks.

3.2   origins and development of UK welfare institutions and the social and demographic contexts in which they have operated
main features of the interrelationship between social policies and differently placed communities, families and individuals

3.3   key concepts and theories of welfare
theories of the state and policymaking
history of contemporary social problems and of social policy responses to them

The content of this chapter is, however, of particular relevance to the following Social Work Subject Benchmarks.

5.1.1 explanations of the links between definitional processes contributing to social differences to the problems of inequality and differential need faced by service users
the social processes that lead to marginalisation, isolation and exclusion

5.1.2 the location of contemporary social work within historical, comparative and global perspectives
the complex relationships between public, social and political philosophies, policies and priorities and the organisation and practice of social work
the significance of legislative and legal frameworks and service delivery standards

Introduction

If Edwardian social policy promoted individual responsibility through the threat of the workhouse, the post-war welfare state demonstrated collective responsibility for the welfare of older people through the 'old people's home' which complemented free access to a full range of healthcare. By contrast, the 1980s demonstrated a sharp move away from institutions generally towards community care based on a mixed economy, a move which has continued until the present. This shift reflected a number of changes and challenges. This chapter focuses on those.

Social policy developments that occurred during that period and post-1997 are connected to some fundamental challenges to the thinking that lay behind the provision of welfare generally, and for older people in particular. In part this was born of a resurgence of liberalism followed by an attempt to find a Third Way under New Labour but in part also there were forces driving the re-evaluation of social services that were beyond politicians' control; demographic trends being chief among these.

Besides exploring those important changes and their causes, this chapter will ask you to develop further the skills which you have now hopefully acquired in connecting social policy initiatives to underlying theories or ideas. In doing so you will need to recall the differences between the prevailing ideology of the Edwardian period covered in Chapter 2 and the justification for the introduction of the comprehensive welfare state covered in Chapter 3. The developments of the 1980s can be seen as a resurgence of liberalism in a more updated form but in another can also be interpreted as an attempt to control state expansion into welfare in a way that fitted with a different economic context. The New Labour 'reforms' reasserted people's rights to services but in a different formulation: one which emphasised choice, the need to avoid social exclusion, and a move away from professionalisation of services in favour of power to consumers (service users) which has culminated in an emphasis on 'personalisation'. This will be explored in greater depth in Chapter 6.

In one sense the rise of the New Right in the 1980s could be seen as an accommodation of the competing theories which we have been studying thus far, with the ensuing New Labour government from 1997 onwards reinterpreting these, yet also reinforcing some of its key elements. To make sense of all of this you will now be required to hone your analytical skills by evaluating the strengths and weaknesses of theories previously explored in a new social context, and then use this analysis to explain current social policy and social work services for older people.

Before doing that, we will need to chart the way in which social work practice changed as a reflection of policy developments in the 1960s and 1970s. Although this book does not look at those two decades in detail, we do need to say something about the developments that took place in this period, as a prelude to an analysis of this chapter's case study, which offers an example of care of older people in the late 1970s. It is important to do this in order to set the scene for the developments that come later.

Cementing and reinforcing the welfare state

The key legislation that established local authority duties towards older people, along with people with disabilities and some specified categories of adults, was the National Assistance Act 1948. This ran in parallel with the duties and responsibilities of the National Health Service, and also, more significantly, in parallel with local authority responsibilities under mental health legislation and the Children Act 1948. Local authorities, required to implement the newly established welfare state system, responded by setting up departments to implement each of these areas of legislation; thus there were local authority children's departments to put the Children Act 1948 into effect and welfare departments to implement the National Assistance Act 1948. In many areas there was a third department which had various names, usually something like a public health department, which incorporated mental health responsibilities along with wider local authority health duties. Furthermore, hospital social work departments were outside all of this. While such a system enabled specialist areas of social work to develop and in some cases to flourish, it had the disadvantage of being a fragmented service, with the result that families could find themselves with two or sometimes even three social workers. A parent with mental health problems, for example, caring for an older relative, could potentially have social workers from the public health department, children's department and the welfare department. Worse still, there could be demarcation disputes: for example, whose responsibility was it to provide support services for parents who had a child with a disability? Disability was formally the responsibility of the welfare departments, yet children clearly came under the aegis of the children's departments.

All of these issues were addressed in the Seebohm Report (1968) from the committee set up as a result of pressure from various quarters, particularly from those who sought the establishment of a family service able to address needs in a more holistic way. In policy terms much of this was driven by a shift in approach to children and young people that drew on therapeutic understandings of their needs, and therefore argued for a more welfare-oriented approach to youth justice and family difficulties. The Ingleby Committee, for example, set up to investigate youth justice and child protection and reporting in 1960, strongly urged this approach.

The outcome of the Seebohm Report was a strong recommendation for a unified, generic department combining the work of three departments in the form of local authority social services departments.

It called for universalism in service provision, seeking to sound the death knell of the stigma and paternalism of the Poor Law legacy, and comprehensive responses to complex needs. It anticipated that organizational unification would result in bigger social work departments in local authorities, with more political influence. At the local level, the Committee advocated area teams, with ten to twelve social workers serving populations of 50,000–100,000, based in neighbourhoods rather than centrally at the town or county hall.

In the main, the Seebohm Report received an enthusiastic reception and it was hailed as a major landmark in social policy, which encapsulated the hopes and wishes of social workers for organizational unification and greater professionalization.

Harris (2008: 670)

The report was implemented through the Local Authority Social Services Act 1970, and subsequently hospital social work was incorporated into the generic departments in 1974. The various professional associations representing the different branches of social work were amalgamated under the British Association of Social Workers, and qualifying courses became generic under the aegis of the Central Council for Education and Training in Social Work, which was established in 1971. This transformation of the social work profession occurred during this period of optimism and enthusiasm for social work, which some have described as its heyday or zenith (Payne 2005: 85). In social policy terms the key developments that had taken place by the mid-1970s were:

- universal provision of services, with some attempt at equalising standards;
- state-run services primarily delivered by local authorities who became the employers of the vast majority of social workers – and consequently the voluntary sector played a lesser role in social work;
- state-financed services with the majority of social services being free, the major exception being means-tested contributions towards the cost of adult residential care.

Applying this specifically to an example of care of older people may help us further to unpack how policy related to social work practice.

CASE STUDY

Women talk about old age

The following is an extract from Ford and Sinclair (1987: 3.1)

Mrs Hatter is nearly 90, small and generally in good health, although slightly deaf in one ear. She lives in an old people's home. Approximately 5% of the population over 65 in United Kingdom live in some form of institution. In the East Midlands, the local authorities provide places in old people's homes for about 15 in every 1000 of those age 65 and over [these figures relate to the early 1980s]. In addition, other people may regularly spend one or two days a week in such homes if day care is provided.

Mrs Hatter's home is purpose built and run by the local authority. They take residents and daycare people, and both men and women. Downstairs there are offices, a kitchen, a large TV room and dining room. Large glass doors lead to a paved area

▶

where people can sit outside if the weather is fine, although the washing is also hung out in this area. Upstairs there are single bed sitting rooms, plus one or two small sitting rooms each with armchairs and a television. One of these sitting rooms belongs (unofficially) to Mrs Hatter and her friend Mrs Mullard, who is older and in poor health and, in Mrs Hatter's view, very depressed and 'a bit of a grumbler these days'. The two women tend to spend their time together there and few other residents intrude. The social worker calls to see them each week, and they really look forward to her visits.

This picture of social work was fairly typical of the 1970s when the welfare state seemed to be continually expanding and social workers were able to visit people living in residential care on a weekly basis. The home offers full-time care to people such as Mrs Hatter and Mrs Mullard and daycare to older people who continue to live in the community supported by family or carers. It represents the best of what was offered at that time: a well-designed environment catering for the needs of nonagenarians which sounds as though it was comfortable and well equipped. It was also typical in that it was run directly by the local authority, as were the majority of residential homes at that time.

Critical thinking exercise 4.1

Compare this description with what you know about care of older people today. If you are not familiar with care provision for older people, you will need to do some research about this.

Answer this in general social policy terms, don't just consider how the regime of the home may have changed.

What are the key differences? What do you think has changed? In what ways does this reflect the social policy context?

Some differences have already been hinted at, but others you may have found more difficult to identify and may have required you to undertake further research. If you have worked with older people or been on placement with an adult care team, you should have found this exercise easier, but see how many differences you managed to identify. Your list may not correspond exactly with what follows but you should be pleased if you have managed to identify at least three broader social policy-related differences.

- The home was run directly by the local authority itself, and although many still are in Britain, they are now in the minority whereas at the time when Mrs Hatter and Mrs Mullard were residents only a very few homes were not local authority-run. Thus one key difference is the way in which residential care is organised and services delivered.

- The degree of social work support offered would take contemporary practitioners by surprise. Firstly, both residents were being visited regularly and frequently – this despite the fact that they are apparently safely and comfortably accommodated and presumably had residential care staff to care for them as well. Secondly, there appears to be no readily discernible reason for the visits, except of course that the residents enjoyed them. In today's social services departments there would have to be a very convincing rationale for this intensity of visiting.
- We can surmise that residential institutions are seen as an important resource and deployed to offer care for people who today would not qualify for residential care. It also seems to be that the residential home is used as a way of supporting people living at home in ways that today might be the prerogative of daycare or community care support services.
- Consequently we could conclude that there does not appear to be the same pressure on resources as there is now and, indeed, once we start to look at demographic data (in Chapter 5) this will confirm that the numbers of older people in their 90s was significantly lower than today even though we are talking of a period just 30 years ago.
- Given little to indicate serious problems – albeit one resident has a slight hearing impairment – contemporary social workers would probably be asking what the justification was for using the expensive resource of residential care. Why are they not both still living in the community? As we shall see, there is now considerable emphasis on people being maintained in the community with residential care only being used as a very last resort for people with very high dependency needs.
- There is therefore now much more emphasis on people living at home and remaining independent for as long as possible. This runs alongside a policy shift away from any form of institutional care towards care in the community. There is a wealth of explanations for this move, some of which we shall explore in this chapter.
- Although not easy to discern this from the case study, one key change has been the introduction of much greater service-user choice which is linked in social work terms to empowerment and in social policy terms to the marketisation of services and, latterly, to personalisation. We shall be exploring marketisation in this chapter and in Chapter 6 focus on personalisation as a key component of current social policy.

We now need to explore these changes, setting them in a social policy context, which means we need to revisit some of the ideas that originally influenced the development of the welfare state.

Challenges to the welfare state: Equality and egalitarianism

This section explains how the whole notion of collective responsibility and state intervention (see Key idea 3.1 in Chapter 3) began to be challenged. It starts by asking you to explore competing views of equality and liberty. It then proceeds to connect those views to different approaches to social welfare, and crucially helps to explain the shifts in policy that occurred in the 1980s, in particular the rise of the New Right and the fundamental challenge to the very ideological base of the welfare state.

Critical thinking exercise 4.2

Look at the following summaries of two contrasting views of equality and liberty, and then draw up a chart that demonstrates the key similarities and differences in approach. You may wish to do this in consultation with student colleagues, or of course, you can carry out this exercise on your own. It is important to try to summarise the key areas in which the views diverge. It would be advisable to consult other social policy texts, or indeed the original works themselves, if you possibly can. This will help you to offer a fully rounded answer, since all that can be offered here is identification of the key points. However, this would be a good starting point if you were ever asked to write an assignment that looked at the underpinning ideology of the welfare state and the challenges mounted to it.

These summaries are extracts from Drake (2001, Chapter 3), but have been subdivided into sections to facilitate consideration of different views. Section 1 clarifies the use of the term 'equality' by Tawney – we examined the views of Tawney briefly in Chapter 3 so it is assumed that you are already familiar with some of his other ideas. The views of Hayek quoted below appeared originally in *The Constitution of Liberty*, which was originally published in 1960.

Section 1
First, 'equality' has been employed in a strict mathematical sense of two or more objects being identical to – or the same as – each other. Second, 'equality' has been used in a social and ethical sense, to the effect that individuals are entitled to equal treatment or consideration when their circumstances coincide.

Equality as an absolute is easy to imagine, but undesirable (and perhaps, impossible) to realise. If absolute equality prevailed, everybody would not only have the same, they would be the same. There could be no differences. Everyone would share identical attributes: the same physiology, the same abilities, energy, resources and aspirations ...

Most egalitarians concede not only that equal shares for all is a utopian idea, but also that equal ability between people is simply not a reflection of real life. People have different skills, talents and amounts of determination, as well as different goals in life. Some work hard, others are lazy; some are serious, others happy-go-lucky; some adventurous, others cautious ... there is a diversity of approaches amongst these supporters of equality which we may characterise as: equality of income, equality of treatment or consideration, equality of opportunity, and equality as individual fulfilment within society.

Tawney attacked the notion of economic equality. His argument, he said, was not for the division of the nation's income into several million fragments, to be distributed without further ado, like a cake at a school treat, equally among all the families. Rather, it was achieved by using tax measures in order to pool surplus resources. These funds could then be used to make accessible to all so as to provide for each, irrespective of income, occupation, or social position, the conditions of civilisation which, 'in the absence of such measures, can be enjoyed only by the rich'... [He] sought practical and feasible movement towards equality and away from what he saw as excessive disparity, and the outcome he desired was the securing of 'a basic minimum below which none should fall', a minimum which would guarantee the essentials of civilised life.

Section 2
Accepting that people had different talents and abilities, [Hayek] argued that equality was incompatible with personal freedom. In Hayek's view, an individual should be free to save or expend his or her resources as he or she pleased ... government should confine itself to developing a framework of law that ensures that the processes of exchange are fair, but should not seek to redistribute wealth to achieve some believed or theoretical notion of social equality. The allocation of wealth should be left to the market ... a free market in which people are at liberty to trade and exchange as they wish. Some will win and some will lose, but the market itself has no intent: it cannot, as an entity, be malign, generous or anything else; the market is not, therefore, an oppressive mechanism. It is like the weather: some will go on holiday and get two weeks of sunshine, others will go another time and receive a fortnight of rain, but the weather itself has not 'decided' who will soak up the sun and who will be drenched.

Section 3
[The liberal view of freedom] is based on negatives, such as the absence of coercion or the avoidance of taxes intended to raise funds for the benefit of others. But egalitarians claim that there are also positive representations of liberty, such as the freedom to work or the freedom to participate in political debate and decision making. In the end, liberty depends on having sufficient economic and social resources in order to exercise choice. If there is no choice, there can be no liberty ...

Neither libertarians nor egalitarians assert or desire the bringing about of freedom or equality in their absolute or unconstrained manifestations. In the heat of political debate, the adherents of both ideologies profess themselves to be against restrictive practices. The targets for egalitarians include the old boy network, freemasonry, and the gentleman's club. Libertarians, on the other hand, demonise the trade union chapel and the closed shop. All these have in common that they provide certain privileges and life chances for some, whilst denying those same opportunities to others.

What did your chart look like? Hopefully something like that in Table 4.1.

Table 4.1

	Tawney	Hayek
Equality, meaning everyone is treated the same	is impossible because it is not a reflection of real life	is impossible because people have different talents and abilities
Equality, meaning everyone should have the same	is not a case of just dividing up a cake, but redistributing resources through taxation	is incompatible with personal freedom so not desirable
Allocation of wealth	should be fairer, with policies directed towards removing disparities	should be left to the market; markets are neutral
Objectives of policy	a minimum which would guarantee the essentials of civilised life	to ensure that individuals should be free to save or expend their resources as they please
Approach to liberty	focuses on positive freedoms such as freedom to work and participate in society	freedom means absence of outside intervention ('negative freedom')
Liberty depends on	having sufficient economic and social resources in order to exercise choice. If there is no choice, there can be no liberty	absence of state intervention and minimal taxation
Chief targets	people who maintain and perpetuate inequality by excluding others, e.g. exclusive clubs and networks	those who interfere in free-market forces such as trade unions

A chart like this is invaluable in helping you to apply key skill 4 – evaluating different perspectives and ideas – to a presentation or written assignment. In presentation terms, a table makes the comparison very clear. There are several points on which Tawney and Hayek disagree, but also a few points of convergence. Similarly, a matrix like this may help you to write an essay since, instead of just describing or narrating one view and then summarising the other, you can engage in a constant compare and contrast approach, using the left-hand column as the topics for each section of the assignment.

Such an approach becomes analytical rather than purely descriptive, and is much more what is required at degree standard.

Returning to our own analysis here, developing the distinction between positive and negative views of freedom further will deepen an understanding of different views of rights, entitlements and justice. The question here is: what are the expectations an individual can justifiably have of the government, and what it is the responsibility of the individual to provide for themselves? There are clearly many different views on this but it might help to elucidate some competing schools of thought. The most extreme on the 'positive rights' side are those held by Marxists, who hold that everyone in society has the right to have their life sustained: to receive according to need, and to give according to ability. The consequence of this would be very extensive government involvement in people's lives. Marxist thinking has exerted a great deal of influence on many aspects of sociology and history as academic studies, but few social policy texts cite Marxism as a direct key influence on social policy decision-making in Britain, so it is not the intention to explore this view in detail here. Other ways of thinking that have been less extreme in their approach have, however, exerted considerable influence.

As examples of this, let's take the different philosophical understandings of entitlements and justice set out by Rawls and Nozick, and the highly influential debate between them that took place in the early 1970s. As we proceed through this comparison of their views you may see some parallels with the thinking of Tawney and Hayek.

Rawls, like Tawney, accepted that some form of inequality is inevitable in society. In *A Theory of Justice* published in 1971, which started the debate with Nozick, Rawls makes five key assumptions about people and about how they enter into a social contract with each other in order to agree how to live. The assumptions are:

- people are self-interested, self-preservation is natural and normal;
- people are equal in the sense that they are equally able and free to debate how society should be run, no one can justifiably claim more power than anyone else;
- people are rational, that is they can think through the consequences of a social contract;
- people have access to information;
- people are ignorant about their own particular futures.

This last point Rawls refers to as the 'veil of ignorance' and it is the key point. In agreeing a social contract, people would be bound to agree on two principles: the principle of liberty whereby people should be allowed to be as free as possible to pursue the kind of life that they wish; and the principle of difference, which assumes that people will have different aims or goals in life and so the social contract must be sufficiently flexible to allow for these differences. Yet because people are ignorant of their particular futures, it is desirable to use a pattern of distribution that most favours the least well-off. This is referred to as the 'maximin' rule of game theory.

It is quite easy to explain this theory. Imagine a board game in which a player has to throw a six to start. The player who throws a six at their first go is like someone who starts life with a large inheritance and wealthy parents. They then progress smoothly and rapidly and often win the game. The player who takes a long time to score the compulsory six before they are allowed to start is like the person who is born into a socially deprived area with parents who face multiple problems including inadequate housing and few social amenities. They progress much later, if at all, and rarely win. This is manifestly unfair and so the 'maximin' strategy ought to be to give everyone the opportunity to play on a relatively equal playing field. In other words, no one should have to throw six to start so that everyone should then have the potential to progress at a relatively equal pace, although of course some will win or do better than others. Therefore, Rawls argues, we are under a moral obligation to assist those who are worse off than ourselves.

Nozick, whose most famous work is *Anarchy, State and Utopia* published in 1974, disputes this saying simply that someone is entitled to have what they have so long as they acquired it legally, or in a way which their society defines as legal. So if you work in something that your society defines as legitimate work, you are entitled to the fruits of your labour. In a just society the three key principles are:

- the just acquisition of what an individual has;
- the just transfer of what an individual has (selling or trading);
- rectification, that is resorting to law if something has been acquired illegally.

If these three key principles are met, that person is entitled to what they have. Other people may be jealous or resent the fact that someone is paid huge amounts of money for being a 'celebrity' on television, or being a 'successful' banker (author's examples, not Nozick's!), but they are not entitled to do anything about it so long as the television celebrity or banker acquired what they have legally. If money or goods are acquired and transferred legally then that society is a just one. There is no greater obligation, except to ourselves. There is certainly no moral requirement to do anything about this. We are moral if we live according to the rules of society. Our prime responsibility is to ourselves as individuals; thus the view that Nozick holds might be described as the extreme of an individualist position.

This is more than just a theoretical philosophical debate. For the debate between the two was played out in social policy in the 1980s and 1990s, and attitudes to policy in relation to older people continue to echo these contrasting views even today. In essence, the views set out by Rawls underpin the notion that society as a whole has a key responsibility for the welfare of all older people in society, whereas those who follow Nozick – usually referred to as the New Right – argue powerfully that it is individuals and their families who have the key responsibility to look after themselves. In the 1980s it is this New Right approach, influenced by Nozick and Hayek among others, that came to dominate social policy.

Challenges to the welfare state: Rethinking the economy

This section explains how core Keynesian beliefs in state intervention in the economy (see Key idea 3.2 in Chapter 3) began to be challenged. It starts with an explanation of monetarism, highlighting the ways in which, as an economic theory, monetarism challenged Keynesian views. It then proceeds to connect the reassertion of belief in free market forces to ideas discussed in the previous section, and this will enable you to understand the rapid move towards a particular approach to community care policies which has dominated social work practice since the 1980s.

The ascendance of the New Right in the late 1970s and 1980s – in the UK generally associated with the Thatcher government, but the movement was replicated throughout much of Europe – was facilitated by changes in economic thinking, and particularly the mounting challenges to Keynesian economics that dominated the welfare state era.

Monetarism, of which the chief exponent is Milton Friedman, takes issue with the way in which Keynesian economics analyses the cause of unemployment and inflation. In brief, monetarism argues that unemployment is caused by people 'pricing themselves out' of the market, asserting that in a properly functioning free market the price of goods and services achieve a level at which they can be successfully bought and sold, without state intervention, and the same argument applies to employment. Interfering with the market, by increasing demand through the government itself purchasing goods or providing more services, necessarily creates a demand for employment but at the expense of causing inflation. Wages and salaries increase since they cannot be regulated by the law of supply and demand, since the government has interfered with this by increasing the demand side, and thus there is high inflation. Monetarism argues that, instead, the concentration should be on the supply side of the equation, rather than the demand side. Thus the state should not involve itself in artificially creating demand, but instead should focus on regulating the supply of money and in this way inflation is limited, prices remain stable, and general prosperity increases. Regulating the money supply means necessarily curtailing public expenditure, reducing taxation, and generally 'rolling back the state'.

This is a very different approach, which clearly will have different outcomes as regards the general role of the state and provision of welfare services. By revisiting the itemised principles of Keynesian economics outlined in Chapter 3 it is possible to tease out these differences and thereby understand the policy changes that reformulated social work in this period.

Critical thinking exercise 4.3

In Table 4.2 on the left-hand side you will see the key elements of Keynesian economic theory, in a very truncated form (to see these in more detail turn back to Chapter 3). Fill in the column on the right-hand side with what you think will be the key differences in a policy that is based on monetarist theory.

Table 4.2

Government should concentrate on the demand side	
Government should invest in public spending to increase employment	
Government should control the amount of currency in circulation or control the rate at which banks lend	
Poverty can be addressed since increasing poorer people's demand for goods and services creates employment	
Redistribution of wealth is desirable if it enables more people to purchase goods and services	
Redistribution can take the form of provision of public services	
Overall, the economy should be a balanced 'mixed economy'	

You will find detailed answers to this exercise at the end of this book. Your answers should certainly have indicated ways in which monetarism struck at the foundation roots of the welfare state, challenging the principles underpinning much of it, and requiring a reformulation of the way in which welfare services including social work would be delivered.

Growth in social work in the 1970s had been facilitated by a commitment to a mixed economy under the overall control of the government with high levels of public expenditure and entitlements to state benefits and state run services. With the return to economic ideas and practices reminiscent of the Edwardian era – indeed the theories are often referred to as 'neoclassical' economic theories, meaning new or revised versions of theories such as those of Adam Smith outlined in Chapter 2 – social work began to change dramatically. It moved from a position of commanding widespread support to one where it was indicative of all that was apparently wrong with the economy and the welfare state. If we connect economists' criticisms of the welfare state with the theoretical debates in the previous section, we will see why and how there was a distinct change in policy and focus for practice.

Social policy and older people in the 1980s: The rise of community care

The 1980s in Britain saw the ascendance of New Right approaches to politics and policy generally. The key feature of social policy as it affected older people at this time was a move away from services provided directly by the welfare state agencies, such as local authorities, toward a more fragmented system and one which emphasised the role of the community. In this section we need to try to connect ideas together to explain this change and the rise of community care.

Critical thinking exercise 4.4

Have a go at answering the following questions:

1. What do you understand by community care?

2. How do you think the move towards community care can be explained by changes in ideas and economic thinking that have been explored so far in this chapter?

In order to complete this exercise you may need to look for definitions of community care and also look back at what we have been studying so far. You then need to map out some connections between the ideas we looked at and what you have discovered about community care.

The discussion which now follows suggests some answers to those questions.

In answer to the first question, it comes as something of a surprise to discover that there is no agreed definition of community care. There is certainly no agreed legal definition despite the fact there is legislation which includes community care in its title (a current example would of course be the National Health Service and Community Care Act 1990). You may have assumed that the term 'community care' implies some kind of agreed collective responsibility for the well-being of people within a given area, but that is not the sense in which it is generally used in social policy. Sharkey (2007: 1), while conceding that it is hard to define community care, suggests that there are three possible interpretations, although these are not mutually exclusive:

- care of people within the community who had previously lived in long-stay institutions;
- efforts made to keep older people, people with disabilities and vulnerable people generally within the community rather than see them go into institutional care;
- the unpaid care and support offered by relatives, friends and neighbours.

In answer to the second question, there are number of ways of connecting the ideas that held sway in the 1980s with community care.

Nozick's contention that *there is no greater obligation except to ourselves* can be interpreted to mean that the primary obligation of each person is to look after themselves and no one has a right to expect other people to look after them or to provide for them, even at a time of need. This does not mean that people should be actively prevented from caring for each other, but rather that no one is entitled to expect others to provide them with an income, pay for services that they might need, and so on. This challenges the fundamental premise on which the welfare state is based, of course. It moves policy away from identifying groups in need and providing services for them towards encouraging people to look after themselves and reducing, or minimising, what the state does. Thus community care in the sense of unpaid care by relatives and others is to be strongly applauded and encouraged.

Reducing state intervention in people's welfare is entirely consistent with monetarist economic theory, since this argues powerfully for a withdrawal of state 'interference' in the operation of the market, and consequent significant reductions in taxation that finance state-provided services. Taxation at levels which financed generous state provision was considered to reduce people's motivation to work since a significant amount of what they earned was given up taxes, so why bother to work? Also high taxation meant that people would be reluctant to invest.

Recalling the debate about the causes of inflation, we can also say that if monetarist interpretations are accepted, this means that public borrowing in order to pay for welfare state services is detrimental to the economy since it fuels inflation, diverting effort away from 'productive' economic activity which is centred on profit-making. The state must therefore look at major reasons for its expenditure. Long-term institutional care would be an obvious target for cuts in expenditure if there were alternatives, especially given that by the 1980s there was a strong body of professional opinion that suggested that many people in long-stay hospitals and homes would be much more appropriately placed in the 'community'.

This challenge to institutional care had started back in the 1960s with the development of ideas of 'normalisation' which originated in challenges to the notion that people with severe learning disabilities (then referred to as 'mentally handicapped') had to be cared for in long-stay hospitals. This had led to a commitment in a number of countries to moving patients or residents out of these long-stay hospitals or homes and back into the community, a process known as deinstitutionalisation.

Optional further study

You will find an interesting summary of these developments in Chapter 2 of **Williams** (2009) and also in Chapter 7 of **Payne** (2005).

For a more detailed and wider-ranging analysis of community care developments as they related to older people, see Chapter 3 of **Lymbery** (2005).

It would be well worth reading one of these chapters.

Although these debates centred on people with learning disabilities or mental health needs, the principle of normalisation extended to all service user groups, so that institutions or residential care came to be seen as a 'last resort' for all people. In our case study earlier in the chapter we encountered two women who appeared to have been placed in residential care almost as a first option, and to some extent this reflected social work practice of the time. However, by the 1980s residential care was no longer seen as a panacea or even as entirely desirable and this applied not just to older people but also to people in all categories of need.

Monetarist belief in free market forces also suggests that services should be provided outside of the state sector, that is by private or voluntary (including charitable) organisations, hence the term 'privatisation' which is used to refer to this process of moving services away from the public sector. Furthermore, monopolistic control by the state of welfare state services left people with few choices, and indeed reduced their capacity to make choices. Instead, those who needed welfare services should be regarded as customers or consumers rather than dependants, and as such they should have the right to choose which services would best meet their own needs. Hence instead of one single provider there should be a multiplicity of providers, each competing to provide the services that people need. Competition would mean that cost of providing services will be determined by the operation of free market forces. Having to pay for services would reduce the demand for them – and promote community care – by building in an incentive for people to remain in their own homes rather than to move to expensive institutional care.

Connecting these ideas drove a strong commitment to 'rolling back the frontiers of the state' which became a mantra of 1980s governments. The state was deemed to be stifling individual effort and interfering too much in matters that were best left to private individuals or families. Indeed politicians argued that there were moral dimensions to this policy.

The welfare state was considered to create dependency, weaken individual morality and undermine the family, with people relying on the state to meet their needs and losing the capacity and/or the will to take care of themselves.

Harris (2008: 672)

Consequently in general social policy terms New Right governments prioritised reducing and controlling public expenditure, moving services deliberately away from the state to the private sector, controlling the money supply in order to reduce inflation, and being prepared to pay the price of a consequential rise in unemployment. As far as social work is concerned, the major implication of such policies is the reduction in the role and power of local authorities and service providers and the emphasis on families taking responsibility for the care of older people and exercising their right to choose when it came to providing themselves any services they thought they needed.

The key question that this inevitably raises is: What role should social work itself play in all this, if any?

Implementing community care

Indeed the debate about whether social work had any role at all was a live one. In 1980 Brewer and Lait published a seminal article posing the blunt question: Can social work survive? This generated a huge amount of controversy at the time. In 1982, by way of an attempt to defuse conflict about the role of social work, seen as increasingly expensive, the Barclay Report promoted the idea of community social work. In some ways this Report could be seen as a way of accommodating social work to New Right views and policies since it promoted the notion that people's needs were best met through informal networks with minimal state provision. Social work did have a role in identifying who was truly in need, and who therefore needed the safety net which was still to be provided by the state. In general terms, social work was to be geared towards encouraging people to develop their potential, to support people in caring for each other, and for encouraging community action. In organisational terms, services would be best provided in small localities, ideally in neighbourhoods, hence community social work. This idea was not widely adopted however, being overtaken by other policy developments.

These other policy developments related to other major concerns. First was the lack of apparent success in the early 1980s in implementing deinstitutionalisation policies in Britain. A report from the House of Commons Select Committee on the Social Services in 1985 drew attention to this lack of progress and a number of initiatives followed that hastened the process of closures, primarily changes in the financial structuring in the NHS. The second major concern, highlighted in the Audit Commission Report of 1986, was an unintended consequence of changes in social security arrangements that coincided with reductions in local authority home care services. This had resulted in a perverse incentive for older people to move into residential homes, since they could then claim social security subsidies once in care. Furthermore, there were major systemic problems that impeded the development of community care, most especially the lack of co-ordinated care arrangements and a funding regime that was confusing and contradictory.

The government took immediate steps to address this by setting up an investigation which resulted in the publication of the Griffiths Report (1988). This recommended that the weaknesses identified by the Audit Commission would be best addressed by giving the local authorities the key co-ordinating role. Griffiths recommended:

 both that local authority social services departments should function as the lead agency for all community care, and that these organisations should develop as enablers and purchasers of care, and hence move away from seeing themselves as monopolistic providers of services, to ensure the continuation of a vibrant independent sector. As a means of controlling the budgets for

> *community care, social services departments were to have the*
> *responsibility for assessing the care needs of any individual who*
> *may be in need of care services.*

Lymbery (2005: 64)

Lymbery goes on to identify a number of weaknesses in the report, including the fact that Griffiths failed to make any proposals for the practical support of carers. The Report also appeared to conflict with the political drive towards reducing local authorities' role generally, but eventually the government conceded this point and introduced legislation that placed the local authority at the centre of the assessment and commissioning process: the National Health Service and Community Care Act 1990.

With implementation of this Act, social work with older people came to be underpinned by two sets of parallel requirements. The first is that local authorities were first and foremost managers of the process. Individuals and families were of course entitled to take whatever action they felt necessary to promote their own welfare needs, but if they could not afford to do so, and sought help from the local authority, then the local authority took over the management of the ensuing procedure. The local authority determines the extent to which that person has needs, as distinct from wants, and it is for the local authority to determine the extent to which the local authority itself would meet the cost of providing for such needs, always operating in the context of service users paying for the services to the extent that they were able (means-testing). The second requirement, which derives from specific requirements in the Act itself, is that local authorities are compelled to become commissioners who purchase services from a variety of potential service providers. This is what came to be known as the 'purchaser–provider split', or 'quasi-market', which requires local authorities to contract out services, and to take responsibility for providing services economically, efficiently and effectively along the lines that were deemed to govern the operation of the private sector.

Optional further study

You will find a much more extensive explanation of the background to community care, together with an assessment of its impact on social work in the 1990s, in Chapter 3 of **Lymbery** (2005).

The National Health Service and Community Care Act 1990 is still the key Act governing social work practice, and is virtually unamended as regards local authority social services departments' role. In effect the system created in the 1980s and early 1990s is the backbone of the system that exists today, although there have been some changes and developments, as you will see in the next section and Chapter 6. However, now would be a good point at which to look back at the ideas discussed earlier in the chapter and see how many of these actually came to be put into practice as policies. In other words, can you relate the theoretical and philosophical challenges outlined earlier in the chapter to the actual practice implemented by New Right governments in the 1980s and early 1990s?

Critical thinking exercise 4.5

Read as widely as you can about the introduction and implementation of community care legislation in the 1990s and answer the following question:

To what extent do community care policies reflect New Right thinking?

This is a topic that could be well set as an essay question. In order to address it, you need to build on the previous critical thinking exercise, and remind yourself of the theoretical challenges to social democratic, Keynesian and the welfare state principles. Then consider which of them were put into practice in actual social policy and which were not.

If you are not sure about the theoretical challenges, you will need to re-read the earlier part of this chapter and possibly Chapter 3.

Combining the ideas of Hayek, Nozick and monetarists such as Friedman, we can see that while some of the challenges are reflected in community care policy, some are not, or at least only to some extent. One good way of answering an essay question would be to group the challenges together as topics and explore the extent to which there have been changes under each topic, and then draw some kind of general conclusion.

The first topic might be freedom. Under this heading we could say that community care policy appears to embody a general acceptance that true equality is not possible and that strong measures to try to achieve equality impede personal freedom. So community care includes an emphasis on people's freedom of choice, freedom to make their own arrangements, and rights to be independent. Yet at the same time we do have a safety net that will offer support services to those in greatest need, and crucially there is widespread acceptance of state-authorised intervention where people are really vulnerable and at risk to themselves. For example, people can be protected from themselves or from others; a recent example of legislation in this area would be the Mental Capacity Act 2005.

The second topic might be marketisation, the emphasis on the free market promoted through encouragement of the private sector and introducing a competitive bidding process through which statutory agencies are obliged to split themselves into smaller competing units. Community care policies certainly created a strong trend in this direction, particularly in relation to care of older people, with a proliferation of private residential care homes, private-sector home care providers and so on. The major compromise accepted by a New Right government was that this market should be organised and mediated through local authorities. The presence of the local authority as a key player with such an important role means that in this sense there is not a totally free market.

The third topic might be reducing taxation. A number of policies designed to try to achieve this included the introduction of charges for services across the board, not just means-tested charging for residential care. This extension was intended to reduce the financial burden on taxpayers. You could also point to the promotion of an ideology that suggests that people should not be a financial burden to others, a clear influence of Nozick. There is a great deal of emphasis on people making proper provision for their own financial futures, and therefore not being dependent on others. However, this had to be achieved through encouragement (and partial subsidy through income tax relief) for people to contribute to private or employer-run pension schemes.

The fourth topic might be the whole idea of 'rolling back the frontiers of the state'. While there was a lot of rhetoric about this, again one could point to the important role of local authorities in service needs assessment as gainsaying this whole notion. Anyone who 'needs' but cannot afford care is, by the National Health Service and Community Care Act 1990, obliged to approach the local authority for a needs assessment. Likewise there was the continuation of the National Health Service as the main provider of primary care services, and this offers the major example of an area in which the frontiers have not been rolled back. Nevertheless, local authorities' roles as direct service providers in social care and social work have been significantly diminished, and the size of the private social care sector would certainly indicate that there has been some reduction in the role of the state. One effect of this has certainly been to diminish the role of trade unions.

Accommodating competing views: The Third Way

The Labour government elected in 1997 committed itself to promoting a Third Way, meaning a route that avoided the extremes of New Right neo-liberalism set against the total state domination of the economy and welfare which proponents of the welfare state seemed to support. It promised *new political responses to meet the needs of modern citizens and social inclusion in a stakeholder society* (Harris 2008: 674). Thus the change of government in 1997 did not bring about any fundamental change in community care policies, or in the arrangement of services for older people generally. There was certainly a change in rhetoric with a move away from the New Right towards the New Labour Third Way, yet the emphasis on value for money, competitiveness, and efficient organisation of services continued to be emphasised.

'Modernisation' was a buzzword used in many policy initiatives, and the context of social work with older people was certainly evident in the 1998 White Paper entitled, predictably, *Modernising Social Services*. This argued for the centrality of quality and service provision rather than a preoccupation with who provides it, and therefore less emphasis on competitive tendering. More generally this was to be achieved through the introduction of the Best Value system, which required evidence that local authorities were delivering what was required, the evidence being the attainment of specified performance targets. The following extract from an editorial that appeared in the *British Journal of Social Work* in 2007 amplifies what this means.

For the development of health and social care, the notion of 'modernization' has a number of particular characteristics:

- the introduction of levers, such as additional pooled budgets available for co-ordinated services, to make progress on collaboration between health and social care agencies;
- changes in the nature of professional working, with particular emphasis being placed on the notion of a 'skills mix', challenging the old-established professional boundaries;
- a simplification of the system of service delivery, such as with the introduction of integrated health and social care facilities within primary care amongst other forms of 'one-stop shop';
- the development of mechanisms that secure a stronger voice for service users in relation to the range of services that are provided;
- the achievement of increased standardization across user/patient groups and geographical areas, with National Service Frameworks being developed to regulate standards and procedures for particular groups of service users/ patients;
- the establishment of detailed systems of performance measurement, seeking to ensure that the overall quality of service can continually be improved;
- a focus on outcomes, ensuring that social care services represent the best possible value for taxpayers' money;
- a pragmatic focus on the development of policies and practices that are most supported by evidence that attests to their effectiveness.

Holloway and **Lymbery** (2007: 379)

Hence one of the series of Frameworks introduced to establish consistency in what families could expect of service providers was the National Service Framework for Older People, published in 2001 (Department of Health 2001; there is a summary of the eight standards in Crawford and Walker 2008: 60–61). Consistency was also to be attained by having some parity concerning how local authorities assess need, and this was to be attained through guidance rather than legislation, in this case in England Fair Access to Care Services published in 2002 (Department of Health 2002; Crawford and Walker 2008: 65–67). The intention of all these policy initiatives was to create a clearer framework of expectations, clarifying the role between the individual and the state, effectively demarcating who was responsible for what. In addition there was an emphasis on equalising services between different areas, making access to services less dependent on what some called a 'postcode lottery' (how good the services are depends on where you live).

The demonstration of the effectiveness of these policies was performance measurement, which involved assessing performance against a range of indicators, priority being given to those that were specific and quantifiable. Some commentators have labelled this as New Labour managerialism which was presented as empowering everyone since its aim was to improve quality standards across the board. This was demonstrated in *A Quality Strategy for Social Care* published in 2000 (Department of Health 2000). This effectively introduced a new layer of accountability with more centralised control over local government reinforced by a regulatory system based on inspections and registration. Registration of the social work workforce itself was introduced by the Care Standards Act 2000 which also covers registration and regulation of all services, public and private. Performance and productivity dominated the organisation of social work services for older people and some say that this has *pushed social work in the direction of narrower approaches to practice* (Harris 2008: 676) while others connect it to deprofessionalisation in which *professional social work is increasingly restricted to a regulatory, service-organising and policing role* (Payne 2005: 105). If you are interested in exploring the impact of performance management on community care there is a specific chapter in Brown (2010) that addresses this.

The notion of individual freedom blends together with the desire for an open market in the emphasis placed recently in policy documents on consumer choice and what has come to be known as 'personalisation' (Department of Health 2005b, 2006; Scottish Executive 2006). In very concise terms this means service users having the rights to have services offered to them that meet their needs and to be able to choose and direct the way in which services are delivered. In order for them to exercise a realistic choice, they need to be confident that the assessments of their needs are consistent, and that the range of services offered will conform to national guidelines and standards; parity of assessment standards is a key feature of *Shaping the Future of Care Together* (Department of Health 2009). Also in order to be able to exercise effective choice, service users must have the right to control the budget that is created following the assessment of need: hence direct payments and individual budgets. Personalisation and all it entails is a theme which will be explored in much more detail in Chapter 6, which offers more information on how this system is designed to work and will explore some research on its implications and effectiveness.

However, in order to round off our discussion of the extent to which theory relates to policy, we need to say something about how the most recent trends in policy related to older people connect with the notion of the Third Way. Do note that, following devolution, the Department of Health documents only technically refer to social work and social care in England, although changes in all four countries have followed similar lines. So wherever you work or study it is worth undertaking the following exercise.

Critical thinking exercise 4.6

In what ways do you think that

1. service user choice

2. national standards

3. performance targets

connect to

1. encouraging people to be as free as possible from state intervention

2. encouraging the use of the market in provision of services

3. encouraging people to look after themselves and avoid being a liability to others?

This exercise is more demanding than it looks for it is not obvious how these interconnect, but Table 4.3 offers some suggestions. There is one suggestion in each box, although you may well have thought of others.

Table 4.3

	Service user choice	National standards	Performance targets
Encouraging people to be as free as possible from state intervention	Users rather than state-employed professionals are responsible for making choices	Means that standards in the private sector equate with those in the public so encourages use of non-state providers	Makes information about non-state providers available and accessible
Encouraging the use of the market in provision of services	Asserts the right for people to choose services from non-state providers	Means that service users can be confident of conformity of standards, so choice becomes a real one	Makes information freely available about the quality of standards offered by various services
Encouraging people to look after themselves and avoid being a liability to others	More empowering, discourages reliance on other people or expecting others to make decisions for people	Clarifies relationship between what people can expect and what state provides so that people do not make unrealistic demands on the state	Establishes criteria by which services are provided, which results in services restricted only to those in most acute need

In all of these ways therefore one could argue that there are aspects of the Third Way that are consistent with New Right thinking. However there are also ways in which they are not. We can demonstrate this by repeating the exercise but with a different task.

Critical thinking exercise 4.7

In what ways do you think that

1. service user choice

2. national standards

3. performance targets

connect to notions of citizenship and positive freedom?

Some suggestions are offered in Table 4.4.

Table 4.4

	Service user choice	National standards	Performance targets
Citizenship	Promotes respect for service users as consumers with rights to exercise choice	Enforces the idea that citizens are entitled to certain basic level of service provision	Enables people to access information to see and check that services meet their requirements
Positive freedom	Promotes the notion of empowerment	Provides a baseline of service expectations to which all are entitled	Lays on local authorities responsibility to ensure that everyone has certain basic needs met

Chapter Summary

In this chapter we have covered a great deal of ground. The chapter began with an explanation of how services developed in the period when the welfare state was established, and how services were reorganised in the early 1970s to provide a unified social work service. We then explored the case study that illustrated social work and social policy as it applied to two women in residential care in this period. This highlighted some key differences between then and now.

We then explored some challenges to the principles that underpinned the welfare state, beginning with notions of equality and liberty, moving on to the extent to which individuals are responsible to each other or to themselves, and then on to challenges to Keynesian economic thinking.

These challenges were accepted and taken on board by governments in the 1980s and 1990s, which moved sharply away from previous policies that encouraged the provision of state-run services. This coincided with the strong international movement towards deinstitutionalisation and community care and influential changes were introduced, principally the National Health Service and Community Care Act 1990.

Having related these back to key aspects of New Right thinking, the concluding part of the chapter examined the attempts to forge a Third Way which brings us up to the change of government in 2010 in terms of contemporary social policy in relation to social work with older people.

The following two chapters explore current policies in greater depth. In the next chapter we look at responses to some specific issues in relation to older people: demographic changes, discrimination, issues of diversity and social exclusion. Then in Chapter 6 we will return to explore personalisation in greater depth, both in order to provide more detail about current policies but also in order to demonstrate how research can help us understand the implications and effectiveness of particular social policy initiatives.

Further reading

Williams, P. (2009) *Social Work with People with Learning Difficulties* (2nd edition). Exeter: Learning Matters.
Chapter 2 provides more on background to deinstitutionalisation and the thinking behind it. Written in the context of learning disabilities, but principles apply equally to older people.
Payne, M. (2005) *The Origins of Social Work: Continuity and Change.* Basingstoke: Palgrave.
Chapter 7 provides more on background to deinstitutionalisation in a general social work context.
Lymbery, M. (2005) *Social Work with Older People.* London: Sage.
Chapter 3 provides a much more extensive explanation of the background to community care than is contained in this chapter, together with an assessment of its impact on social work in the 1990s.
Sharkey, P. (2007) *The Essentials of Community Care* (2nd edition). Basingstoke: Palgrave.
Provides a good, general overview of current community care policy and practice.
Brown, K. (2010) *Vulnerable Adults and Community Care* (2nd edition). Learning Matters: Exeter.
Essential reading for Post-Qualifying social work students specialising in working with adults.
The following are all government policy documents relevant to this chapter, available through the Department of Health website (**www.dh.gov.uk**):
Department of Health (1998) *Modernising Social Services*
Department of Health (2000) *A Quality Strategy for Social Care*
Department of Health (2001) *National Service Framework for Older People*
Department of Health (2002) *Fair Access to Care Services*
Department of Health (2005) *Independence Well-being and Choice: Our vision for the future of social care for adults in England*
Department of Health (2006) *Our Health, Our Care, Our Say*
Department of Health (2009) *Shaping the Future of Care Together*

5 The Lived Experience of Older People in Britain: **Demographics and Diversity**

Dawn Ludick and Robert Johns

Introduction

This chapter moves away from the more theoretical constructs and ideas underpinning
social policy generally towards consideration of some specific challenges for social
policy presented by older people. In particular, this chapter highlights the social policy
challenges of responding to the needs of specific groups of older people, groups that
either share a common identity or who experience certain forms of disadvantage or

oppression. It starts by investigating demographic trends that will have a real impact on social policy, for not only is the overall number of older people increasing, but also there are changes in relation to specific subgroups within the older age group. It then moves on to an exposition of research and evidence concerning the needs of the older population. It concludes by connecting these needs to the competing theoretical ideas and ideologies that were outlined in Chapters 2–4.

This chapter will require you to develop some skills in evaluating research evidence, an essential requirement for level 3 of any undergraduate degree, absolutely essential in any postgraduate degree, and also an important prerequisite for engaging in sound evidence-based social work practice.

The purpose of this chapter is to explore those aspects of the lived experience of older people in contemporary Britain that are relevant to social policy. The focus is on older people's special needs, addressed through a set of questions which we will address in various ways right through the chapter.

- What changes are occurring in relation to the older population of which policymakers need to be aware?
- What challenges confront policymakers trying to address the needs of older people generally? Specifically, as it is of particular relevance to social work, in what ways does social policy connect to issues of diversity and discrimination related to older people?

CASE STUDY

Mary Nowak is 68 years old. As her name might suggest, she has Polish connections. Her husband's father moved to Britain during the Second World War to help with the war effort and stayed there once the war ended. However, her own family have always lived in Britain for as long as anyone can remember. She would describe herself as white British if asked.

She and Jozef lived most of their life in Haltenford, where his parents lived and where their daughter now lives (they had one child). However, when Jozef retired from the local brickworks 10 years ago they put into effect his dream to move to a small house in a country village. Just 12 months after moving, Jozef died but Mary decided to stay there as she had an interesting office job in a town five miles from where they lived. Mary's intention was to carry on working as she needed the social contact the office provided, as well as much-needed income, but as soon as she attained the age of 65 the firm insisted that she retire. She did not have an occupational pension so is now dependant on the state pension and her savings, which are fast running out. Worsening arthritis in her legs obliged her to sell her car and she became reliant on the infrequent bus service to get to the local town to access shops and amenities.

> She has found it very difficult to cope on her own, feeling very isolated despite occasional visits from her daughter who lives at Haltenford, 30 miles away. She has been prescribed medication by her GP both for her depression and to help with the pain which the arthritis causes.

- What are the different groups and different sets of needs within the older population?
- What are the principal issues that social policy needs to address in order to meet the needs of older people?

The first of our critical thinking exercises in this chapter asks you to think about the areas of social policy that are relevant to this case study. You are not going to be asked what you would do about the case as a social work or social care practitioner, but instead to identify ways in which the lived realities of Mary's life touch on social policy issues. Here we do mean social policy as distinct from social work practice; there are a number of practice-related and organisational issues you could identify, but these are not our concern here. If you need further guidance on this you may want to look in particular at the case study and associated activities in Chapter 7 of Crawford and Walker (2008: 157); there are some deliberate similarities with that case study.

Critical thinking exercise 5.1

Looking at the case study above, what areas of social policy appear to you to be relevant? List some broad headings, rather than detailed specific points.

There are number of ways of tackling this task, but one logical method would be to proceed through the case study stage by stage, categorising the various factors together.

The first point you should have noted is that Mary has a particular identity defined both in terms of her gender and ethnicity as well as her age. It is all too easy to focus just on people's chronological age, without taking into account their personal histories and identities. Such an approach would be discriminatory; it simply takes one fact about someone – their age – and builds on it a set of assumptions about their needs and requirements. In this sense age discrimination has some similarities with other forms of discrimination, such as race, gender, disability or sexuality. So before a systematic analysis of policy can be undertaken, we need information about the subgroups that comprise older people, and need to start to consider the extent to which policies are responsive to the needs of particular groups of people rather than just older people generally.

The second point you may have noted concerns employment and possible discrimination. Despite the fact that she clearly would have wanted to carry on working, Mary was compelled to retire at the age of 65. One might reasonably ask what laws and policies exist to prevent this happening. Is it right that someone can be effectively dismissed just because of their age? This might lead us to reflect further on policies more generally in relation to age discrimination. What are the other relevant issues in relation to age discrimination?

Leading on from this, you may also have noticed one consequence of this loss of employment: less mobility and increasing isolation. Comparative geographical remoteness has now translated into a form of social exclusion, with a consequent effect on access to support. It is extraordinary how popular 'location' television programmes have become: that is the kind of programme that encourages people to move homes, often to a completely different area, and evaluate the proposed move purely in terms of the amenities the new house potentially offers, without taking into account any consideration access to amenities, the nature of the local community or the potential for developing new social networks. In this particular case moving away from the town in which relatives lived seems to have had detrimental consequences, although initially it sounded like the fulfilment of a dream.

The fourth point, somewhat related, concerns poverty. Often in the UK, as a result of loss of employment, older people experience a substantial fall in their income. If we survey the evidence of the number of older people who are in relative poverty, we quickly discover that there is a comparatively high percentage of older people over pension age who are below the generally agreed 'poverty line'. Poverty can also be used in a broader sense, referring not just to people's income but also to their general standard of living and well-being, for example the quality of housing, heating, nutrition, and healthcare. The multiplicity of factors connected to poverty can result in more general social exclusion and it will be interesting to note the extent to which policymakers have addressed social exclusion in the context of older people.

The fifth point relates specifically to health. You will have noticed in the case study that Mary has a combination of a physical disability (her arthritis) and potential mental health needs in relation to her depression. Disability and impairments are major features in the lives of many older people and depression among older people may be much more common than is supposed (Crawford and Walker 2008: 110–115, 80).

This leads on to the final sixth point, who cares for older people with disabilities or particular needs? We have already seen that community care policies fit well with some approaches to social policy generally, especially where they emphasise the responsibilities of families and informal carers. What may not have been realised is that many older people are carers themselves, caring for a partner or in some cases children in their 60s or 70s caring for a parent. So we need to pay some attention here to policies that focus on older carers' needs.

In the next part of the chapter we shall explore the six points listed above in more detail. The intention is to offer a brief summary of some of the evidence of need, to indicate areas that social policy needs to address, and suggest where you might go to find more information. This will enable us in the final section of the chapter to revisit the different theoretical perspectives explored thus far in this book in order to indicate how policymakers might respond. In the following chapter we can then explore in some detail the most recent trend in social policy that attempts to respond to the diversity of older people's needs, personalisation.

For the sake of clarity, the six areas indicated above will comprise the next six subheadings under the titles: diversity, age discrimination, social exclusion, poverty, health and carers. Needless to say, this does not imply that they are in any order of priority, nor are they necessarily totally comprehensive. For example, there are important social work practice considerations in relation to the protection of vulnerable older people from various forms of abuse, but these are not given detailed consideration here since the intention is to focus on those areas where there are fundamental differences of social policy approach.

Diversity

In this section we start with some general information about the constitution of the older population in Britain today. We then consider research concerning specific identified groups.

The following information comes from the Office of National Statistics (ONS) and the figures cited relate to the year 2008. If you want more detailed or up-to-date information, it is well worth visiting the ONS website (for address see end of chapter).

Table 5.1 shows projected population by age to 2033.

Research summary

Source: Office of National Statistics 2008

There were 19.8 million people aged 50 and over in the United Kingdom in 2002. This was a 24 per cent increase over four decades, from 16.0 million in 1961.

The improvement in death rates among older men has led to a narrowing of the gap. There were 28 per cent more women than men aged 50 and over in 1961, but only 18 per cent more in 2002.

Up to the age of around 70, the number of males and females are fairly equal. The ratio of females to males increases progressively from 1.1 at age 71, to 2.1 by the age of 89. This reflects the higher life expectancy of women at older ages and higher male mortality during the Second World War.

The median age for women (40 years) was higher than for men (38 years). This is because, on average, women live longer than men.

Table 5.1: Projected population by age, United Kingdom, 2008 to 2033 (millions)

Age \ Year	2008	2013	2018	2023	2028	2033
0–14	10.8	11.0	11.5	11.9	11.9	12.0
15–29	12.3	12.7	12.3	12.1	12.3	12.8
30–44	13.0	12.5	12.8	13.8	14.2	13.8
45–59	11.8	12.7	13.2	12.6	12.2	12.5
60–74	8.8	9.4	10.0	10.5	11.4	11.9
75–84	3.4	3.7	4.0	4.8	5.2	5.3
85 and over	1.3	1.5	1.8	2.2	2.6	3.3

Over the last 25 years the percentage of the population aged 65 and over increased from 15 per cent in 1983 to 16 per cent in 2008, an increase of 1.5 million people in this age group. Over the same period, the percentage of the population aged 16 and under decreased from 21 per cent to 19 per cent. This trend is projected to continue. By 2033, 23 per cent of the population will be aged 65 and over compared to 18 per cent aged 16 or younger.

The fastest population increase has been in the number of those aged 85 and over, the 'oldest old'. In 1983, there were just over 600,000 people in the UK aged 85 and over. Since then the numbers have more than doubled, reaching 1.3 million in 2008. By 2033 the number of people aged 85 and over is projected to more than double again to reach 3.2 million, and to account for 5 per cent of the total population. The number of people aged 90 and above is projected to more than triple by 2033, the number of people aged 95 and over is projected to more than quadruple, and the number of centenarians is projected to rise from 11,000 in 2008 to 80,000 in 2033, a more than sevenfold increase.

It is anticipated that the ratio between the working-age population and the retired population currently at 3.23 will decrease to 2.78 by 2033.

So in our case study Mary being the survivor of the partnership is, statistically, a more common event than the man being left alone, but she potentially has many more years to live. There is an imbalance in gender proportions, with more women than men living longer; the ONS estimate that by 2033 the proportion of women to men will be 117:100.

You will also notice from these figures that the proportion of older people is increasing in comparison with younger people, that is, progressively there are more older people and fewer young people. This means that there will be a smaller number of working-aged people relative to the retired population and therefore there will be less money to support a greater number of older people, particularly the very old, than is currently the case.

Critical thinking exercise 5.2

Why does this matter? What are the social policy implications? What policies might ensue?

If you found it difficult to work this out straight away, think about potential sources of finance for the services older people need. If these are to be paid for by the state, money for them has to be found from taxation, and one major source of taxation comes from income tax paid predominantly by people in employment, although people do pay tax on their pensions as well – a point often forgotten by the media. So, assuming that it is by and large younger people who are in employment and older people who are not:

- if the proportion of older people in the population increases, so will the demand for services; yet at the same time
- if the proportion of younger people in the population decreases, there will be fewer people to pay for the services older people need;
- consequently, not only does the absolute cost of services rise, but those costs have to be shared by fewer people, so there needs to be a proportionate increase in taxation to compensate for this.

There are a number of social policy strategies that could be devised to address this besides simply increasing the amount of taxes levied. Here are some examples.

- One would be to reduce the demand for services by redefining needs and entitlement to services.
- Another would be to transfer services from the public sector to the private so that they were no longer financed through taxation with people expected to pay for themselves – although what happens if they cannot afford to do so?
- A third would be to decrease the proportion of older people by redefining what qualifies as 'older' – this is not as silly as it sounds, since if it were possible to increase the pension age whereby people are defined as 'old', not only would this reduce the proportion of older people numerically (theoretically) but more importantly it would transfer some of the non-working population to the working population.

By way of demonstration that the last point is being seriously considered read the following quotations.

 From 6 April 2020 the State Pension age will be 65 for both men and women. Between 2024 and 2046 the State Pension age will increase for both men and women. This increase will be gradual, happening over two years every decade. The changes will mean that:

> State Pension age for men and women will increase from 65 to 66 between April 2024 and April 2026
>
> State Pension age for men and women will increase from 66 to 67 between April 2034 and April 2036
>
> State Pension age for men and women will increase from 67 to 68 between April 2044 and April 2046

The quotations above are all from **Directgov** 2010 online.

> *Our societies will need to adjust to having more older people, which has implications ranging from pensions provision to the design and funding of essential services such as care and health. But personal adjustments will be just as important: individuals need to prepare for longer working lives and longer retirement.*
>
> **Harrop** and **Jopling** (2009: 10)

> *We agree that there is a need to explore options for the long term funding of the care and support system, to ensure that it is fair, sustainable and unambiguous about the respective responsibilities of the state, family and individual.*
>
> **HM Government** (2007: 1)

> *For the individuals themselves the future may hold two or more decades of retirement or semi retirement, many in this survey would appear to have the financial resources to lead a secure old age, but there will be large numbers of these aging baby boomers, increasingly being supported by their children and grandchildren who will need to work until their late 60s to contribute to the health and other needs of the boomers*
>
> *[People who retire] may have difficulties in adjusting to a life without a clear occupation and 'identity'.*
>
> **Christopoulos** and **Bromage** (2009: 65)

Thus far we have been talking about older people as if they were one homogenous group. Indeed policymakers often go no further than this, overlooking the important point that within the older age group – as in all age groups – there are many different groups with different needs.

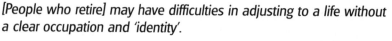

Critical thinking exercise 5.3

What different groups of older people are there? Why does this matter? What are the social policy implications?

While there are all sorts of potential ways of distinguishing different groups of older people, the intention here is to focus on key differences so the discussion that follows concentrates on black and minority ethnic (BME) and gay and lesbian elders.

Black and minority ethnic (BME) elders

There is a wealth of information to demonstrate that there are a significant number of BME older people living in the UK. ✗

The 2001 census revealed the following data analysed by the Office for National Statistics.

> ### Research summary
>
> *In 2001, 15 per cent of people from non-White minority ethnic groups were aged 50 and over (around 672,000 ✗ people). This compares with 33 per cent of the overall population.*
>
> *Black Caribbeans have the oldest age structure of all the non-White ethnic groups – 24 per cent were aged 50 and over. The Mixed group had the youngest age structure, with just under 8 per cent aged 50 and over.*
>
> The 2010 **Office for National Statistics** update states:
>
> *The number of people aged 85 and over in the UK reached 1.3 million in mid-2008, accounting for 2 per cent of the population compared with 1 per cent in 1971.*
>
> *There were more than twice as many women aged 85 and over than men: 914,000 compared with 422,000.*
>
> *The proportion of people aged 85 and over is projected to increase further, to reach 4 per cent by 2031.*
>
> *In mid-2008 the proportion of the UK population over state pension age, 65 for men and 60 for women, was 19 per cent, equivalent to 11.8 million people.*

The ONS have produced a table which shows the proportion of older people in specific ethnic minority groups. See Table 5.2.

Table 5.2: Percentage of older people in each ethnic group, Census 2001

		65–84	85+
White	British	14.9	2.1
	Irish	22.9	1.9
	Other	9.5	0.9
	ALL	14.9	2.1
Mixed	ALL	2.7	0.3
Asian	Indian	6.2	0.3
	Pakistani	3.9	0.2
	Bangladeshi	3.1	0.1
	Other Asian	4.9	0.3
	ALL	5.0	0.3
Black	Black Caribbean	10.2	0.4
	Black African	2.2	0.1
	Other Black	3.0	0.3
	ALL	6.2	0.3
Chinese	ALL	4.8	0.3
Other ethnic groups		2.7	0.2
ALL non-white minority ethnic population		4.8	0.3
ALL POPULATION		14.0	1.9

Critical thinking exercise 5.4

What conclusions can you draw from these data? Just spend a few moments thinking about it before reading the next paragraph.

From this we can conclude that, generally speaking, the proportion of white people aged 85+ as a proportion of all white people is much higher than the equivalent Asian or black groups. However, non-white groups are among the fastest-ageing population groups, and are destined to comprise a growing proportion of the older population as the overall population ages in the next 10–15 years (Zahno and Rhule, 2008). McIntosh (2008:1) estimates a 170 per cent increase between 2005 and 2012. *Sure Start to Later Life* (Department of Work and Pensions, 2006: 102) suggests that the ethnic minority older population will rise from 175,000 to over 1.8 million by 2026.

These demographic changes need to be taken into consideration as service provision for older people is planned with both national and local services devised to provide services which cater for a diverse aging population (Zahno and Rhule, 2008: 9; Department of Work and Pensions, 2006: 102). More specifically, Zahno and Rhule (2008) highlight some of the most significant needs of BME older people; these include health, housing, social support networks and finances, as well as the uptake of service provision.

Yet we must bear in mind that people's circumstances have been affected by numerous realities such as the time period and the way in which they might have immigrated to the UK. For example, there will be very different needs between BME old people who have lived in the UK for a long time compared with those who have had a difficult immigration process in recent years. This immigration might have involved fleeing persecution from their country of origin; during the actual journey to the UK they may have encountered various challenges and even traumatic experiences. The perceptions they might have had of what it would be like arriving in the UK and the actual reception they experienced on arrival in the UK will have an impact. Furthermore, their experiences may have been compounded by language barriers and education, and these factors may impede their potential ability to access services. McIntosh (2008) highlights how BME old people might feel a sense of shame and fear being misunderstood if they were to ask for help, suggesting that they may also face discrimination through a combination of age, ethnicity and mental health.

Some of the discrimination which exists may derive from the stereotyping of various cultures without taking into consideration the emerging changes which might be accruing for those particular groups. For instance, as different groups develop their own mechanisms for integration into British society they may begin to adapt to some of the values and customs which may not have been part of their culture of origin. An expectation of care of elders within the extended family, for example, may have been an intrinsic element of the originating culture but is lost in the adaptation to life in Britain. As evidence of this, Zahno and Rhule (2008) found that despite certain ethnic minority groups living in extended families comprising several generations, other members in the family may often not be fully aware of the old person's care needs or how to access benefit entitlements such as direct payments or aids and adaptations. There may, of course, be other reasons to which failure to access entitlements can be attributed: the sheer complexity of the system found to be bewildering, English not being the first language, or the lack of a National Insurance number, for example.

The first social policy implication therefore would be an examination of the current provision and the extent to which it was sensitive to people's cultural background. This needs to start with information about the range of different cultures to which BME elders belong and a thorough knowledge of their reality. It is clearly of the utmost importance to establish strong links between BME community groups and mainstream service provision.

The second implication concerns equality of access to services. Quality service provision *includes acknowledging ethnic diversity, ensuring equal access, delivery and continuous care for all older people, regardless of ethnic minority status* (Mold, Fitzpatrick and Roberts, 2005: 107). The range of services needs to take into consideration the language, cultural and religious differences of the BME community. Often the cultural and religious customs are firmly embedded in the day-to-day living arrangements; so social work and social care services need to reflect this.

Looking more specifically at some illustrations of providing culturally sensitive services, these might include:

- ensuring that appropriate places of worship of different faiths are accessible to people for whom this is important;
- providing music which is appropriate and a reminder of the past as well as providing traditional food;
- paying attention to gender issues if this is of importance to the ethnic minority population group; for example, it may be a cultural expectation that personal care is provided by staff of the same gender as the older service user.
- basic essential information translated into the appropriate language which is then followed up with professional workers who are able to discuss key concepts in ways which the person is able to understand (Zahno and Rhule, 2008: 5);
- an awareness of whether ethnic groups actually read the information translated or whether people tend to rely more on information been passed down through discussions;
- the use of translators who have a clear understanding of social and healthcare provision so as to overcome barriers where words like 'care' might not be used in certain ethnic minority groups (Netto 1998: 223);
- the profile of staff working in social care and health reflecting the ethnicities of the groups they are supporting.

Netto (1998: 225) suggests that a proactive approach needs to be taken in the service provision for ethnic minority groups. The services need to take into consideration the cultural isolation which can be experienced. She suggests that health professions who come into contact with older people and their carers can support the raising of awareness of services available.

'Gay greys'

This term is being used here to refer to gay and lesbian older people, which here also includes bisexual and transsexual people. In contrast to ethnicity, obtaining statistical information about the numbers of gay and lesbian older people is notoriously difficult. In truth, as Musingarimi (2008) points out, numbers can be no more than estimates since many older people may not be open about their sexual orientation and, even if asked, might deny it. Many older people were, after all, brought up in an era when homosexuality was illegal and classified as a mental disorder. Furthermore, while many surveys have questions concerning gender and ethnicity, very few include sexual orientation; the national census data, for example, does not. Despite these shortcomings, it is estimated that approximately 5–7 per cent of the population are lesbian, gay or bisexual and presumably the proportion of the older population would be roughly the same. This means that, on current projections, by 2031 there could be as many as 1 to 1.4 million gay, lesbian and bisexual people aged 60 and over in the UK (Musingarimi, 2008: 3–4).

A Sure Start to Later Life (Department of Work and Pensions 2006: 103) highlights how older gay people fear the negative responses they may face when their sexual orientation becomes evident in the light of 'transitions' which may arise from poor health such as requiring hospitalisation or through the need for additional support within their own home from carers.

 These women and men have lived through some of the most significant years in terms of gay history and social change, including the declassification of homosexuality as a mental illness, the decriminalization of homosexuality and the appearance of AIDS.

Concannon (2009: 404)

Concannon also highlights how services have been developed around heterosexual white British families.

With the inception of the Civil Partnership Act 2005, there have been some improvements for same-sex couples as their partnership is considered legal and this has impacted positively on entitlements to pension, benefits and inheritance.

Despite these changes, gay people may still face prejudice, even from professional health and social care staff. Langley (2001) cites an example of some of the prejudices discovered with a same-sex couple who had been together for 50 years. One partner was disabled; the non-disabled partner was referred as being disruptive when found sharing the same bed as her partner. They had been ridiculed and belittled by staff. One patient had been accused of taking sexual advantage of her confused and vulnerable roommate, who was in fact not confused, but unable to speak because of her stroke (Langley 2001: 929).

Later Life as an Older Lesbian, Gay or Bisexual Person (Age Concern 2008) provides another case vignette which illustrates some of the prejudices encountered:

 My home care worker said she was unhappy about washing me after I had cut myself shaving as she thought I might have AIDS. She has also insinuated in the past that I must be a paedophile just because I am a gay man. I found myself dreading her visits because she is so obviously homophobic.

Age Concern (2008: 14)

Langley (2001) reminds us that gay older people might require services for the very same reasons as would heterosexual old people: illness, frailty, disability, life transition. Services required need to be viewed *in the context of [their] particular needs, vulnerabilities and strengths* (Langley, 2001: 917). Such older people are less likely to have children; as they age, their network will be different from heterosexual old people or possibly even lacking. Despite having been previously married and having children before 'coming out', lesbian old people might be estranged from their children, while gay men are less likely to have children (Musingarimi, 2008: 3). Consequently, gay people are more likely to turn to professionals for help and therefore discriminatory prejudices within services need to be challenged.

Concannon (2009: 405) highlights some of the ways in which practice might continue to discriminate against gay people; for example, a simple question about marital status as either single or married on an admission form dismisses some older people's sexual history. Often there is the assumption that accommodating gay people in service provision is only about the sexual aspect of an older person's life. However, being gay or lesbian shapes the person's entire experience in terms of their friendships, interests, and social networks (Lishman 2006). Gay people need the assurance that services they receive allow them to be themselves and they are safe from discrimination and stigma. In social policy terms, organisations have to change in order to be responsive to all service users, rather than potential recipients of services having to adjust to what is available 'mainstream'.

 It is the organisation that needs to 'come out' as gay or lesbian friendly rather than depending upon clients to 'come out' in order to get their needs met.

Lishman (2006: 7)

Age discrimination

Critical thinking exercise 5.5

How can social policy address general discrimination against older people? Are there any policy changes that need to be implemented in order to address age discrimination?

You could attempt to answer this by drawing up a plan for an assignment on this topic, in which case you would need to start with the evidence that there is discrimination before outlining specific areas in which you consider that social policy needs to be directed or reorientated in order to address discrimination.

A good starting point in tackling discrimination would be to start with ourselves as (hopefully open-minded) students of social policy. We need to reflect on our own perceptions and attitudes, which immediately leads us to consider the experiences that have influenced us. Then we need to think about the attitudes demonstrated in other professionals' practice and in society in general. For further information and some useful exercises on this see Chapter 1 of Crawford and Walker (2008) or Banks (2006).

We might also consider why there is discrimination against older people. After all, becoming older is (hopefully) an aspect of everyone's life. So it may not be discrimination based on perceived differences, yet few would deny that older people are seen at least to some extent as a liability, as dependants, as a 'problem'. One explanatory suggestion is that we live in a society which places a high value on independence as an important indicator of adulthood. Independence for us can be the ability to care for ourselves; is it that we find facing old age challenging, when we reconsider the notion of once again becoming dependent and unable to do some of the things we once were able to do? Whatever the reason, we need to understand what underpins it and seek to identify the paradigm shifts which need to be made in order to ensure older people are treated fairly and receive the services they need.

Next we need to investigate the extent of discrimination. Harrop and Jopling (2009: 13, 18) highlight the extent to which older people experience age discrimination as an everyday occurrence in their life, with 60 per cent of people aged over 65 believing that age discrimination affects older people's everyday lives, with just as many identifying it in the workplace. They suggest that all services need to be 'age-proof' and allow for age equality. This can be addressed by ensuring that there is a heightened awareness of age discrimination law. Some of the ways in which this is envisaged is of older workers receiving equal redundancy packages and more flexible working opportunities with support in making transitions and adaptations to the technological age.

Yet this is a far cry from the current position. For example, the Employment Equality (Age) Regulations 2006 implemented the European Directive outlawing age discrimination in employment and vocational training. However, the government restricted the protection available to people over the age of 65 by creating a new 'default retirement age' of 65 for both men and women. This permits employers to set a mandatory retirement age at or above the age of 65, which means that an employer can compel employees to retire at 65 and can refuse to recruit anyone over the age of 65, providing they follow the correct procedure. This policy was challenged by Age Concern and Help the Aged (now Age UK), who sought a judicial review which eventually ended up being referred to the European Court of Justice, who confirmed that it was lawful for the UK government to set a default retirement age providing it was justified on grounds of social or employment policy (R (on the application of Age UK) v Secretary of State for Business, Innovation & Skills [2009] EWHC 2336).

So, ironically, age discrimination becomes officially sanctioned. However, one way in which policy could be changed – and at the time of writing this is under active consideration – would be for the government to scrap all mandatory retirement ages and simply let people decide for themselves when to retire. Presumably many people's decision will be influenced by the age at which they could claim a pension of some sorts, but effectively the official policy would be that people can carry on in employment until they themselves decide not to.

There may be other areas which you have identified in which there is discrimination and the need for policy changes at the macro or wider level. However, the discussion here will now turn to one specific area of experience for older people, mainly as consumers of care services, focusing on residential care.

Despite an estimated 410,000 older people living in 15,700 care homes, Scourfield (2007: 1136) suggests there is still stigmatisation associated with residential homes as the 'last refuge' where people remain until they die. Furthermore:

 It is often assumed that when someone enters residential care, their disability or illness is so all-consuming that they have no interest in anything other than their personal care and their day-to-day comfort.

Scourfield (2007: 1136)

Scourfield goes on to suggest that residents may have restricted communication and cognitive abilities yet feel reliant on the personal relationship with residential staff to ensure that their needs are met; this often leaves them feeling vulnerable and concerned that any concerns they might express will impact on their care. The policy challenge therefore is to ensure that old people in residential care have access to the information they need and a voice in the services they receive. One response, Scourfield suggests, is to acknowledge the importance of not reducing old people to 'service users' but to take care to remember that residents are still citizens.

This analysis is echoed in the research which is summarised in the Social Care Institute for Excellence (SCIE) adult services guide *Dignity in Care* (Cass, Robbins, and Richardson 2009). If you are a social work practitioner it is well worth while reading this report in full. The research summary suggests that respect for personal identity is a major factor in older people's lives, and one which is often overlooked. It then looks at a number of areas relevant to promoting dignity and countering or avoiding discrimination, for example:

- avoidance of patronising attitudes and encouraging professionals to treat service users as equals;
- improved communication so that older people know what is happening to them;
- helping people maintain links with their communities;
- promoting independence, particularly into choice and direct payments (direct payments will be covered in more detail in Chapter 6);
- respecting people's rights to privacy and confidentiality;
- helping people to maintain their personal appearance.

While some of these may appear comparatively minor issues, they are of great importance to the individuals concerned and so one key social policy principle to draw from all of this is that all social policy should be examined in terms of the effects it will have on older people, not just generally, but in relation to their individual experiences as individual citizens, as consumers of services, but also as people who participate in society. As we saw in previous chapters, there are a number of different views about how you promote this participation and whether this argues for greater or lesser state involvement in people's lives. We will return to this point at the end of this chapter and again in Chapter 6.

Social exclusion

Critical thinking exercise 5.6

How do you think the concept of social exclusion applies to older people?

You may need to start by reminding yourself of definitions of social exclusion. A good way for this is to think about the everyday experiences of older people, and then to think of ways in which they may be excluded from society.

The English Longitudinal Study of Ageing (Banks et al. 2008) is based on follow-through research of a cohort of people as they progress through old age. The most recent study reported on a four-year follow-up of the original cohort and yielded a great deal of useful information on several aspects of ageing. One important element of the research is social exclusion and what the researchers call 'social detachment'. What follows is a summary of the findings.

Research summary

Approximately half of older people were at risk of social detachment and around 7 per cent showed signs of social detachment at a given point in time.

The duration of social detachment does matter: quality of life consistently reduces with the duration of social detachment.

The characteristics most strongly associated with a longer duration of social detachment were those related to family composition, specifically not living with a partner. Older people living alone, those living with their children only (i.e. without a partner) and those living with other people but not with partner or children were at risk of longer-lasting social detachment.

Other demographic characteristics that increase the odds of sustained social detachment include having a low level of education and being male.

The odds of being persistently detached were three times higher for those reporting poor health than for those reporting excellent health.

Older people on low income, those suffering from material deprivation and those living in poor housing were markedly more likely to be affected by longer-lasting social detachment.

Older people who lacked access to various services, transport, financial products or modern communication technologies faced an increased risk of prolonged social detachment.

Age itself has been found not to have an independent effect on the persistence of social detachment.

A survey of 1000 people carried out for Age Concern in 2004 (Age Concern online) revealed the following.

One in five people over 65 are alone for more than 12 hours a day.

Those over the age of 65 are twice as likely as other age groups to spend over 21 hours of the day alone.

These people are more at risk of depression and ill-health caused by isolation and loneliness.

More than a quarter of people over 65 do not have a best friend, which is higher than any other age group.

A third of people over 65 see their local supermarket as somewhere to socialise and get out of the house and one in five people eat their meals there rather than at home.

Over 3.5 million older people live alone and many do not have regular visitors or any opportunity to get out of the house.

As to the causes, the government document *Sure Start to Later Life – Ending Inequalities of Older People* (Department of Work and Pensions 2006) highlights three. First, if people are experiencing exclusion in their mid-life there is the likelihood that this will continue into old age. Second, there are significant events which are more likely to be experienced in old age which can further encourage social exclusion, such as bereavement, lack of employment, illness, mental health, fragility, fear (real or perceived) of the environment in which people live, experience of crime. Finally, the impact of age discrimination should not be underestimated as this influences both the aspirations of individuals and the environment within which they operate. The document also surmises that there can be an attitude which suggests that certain events are 'inevitable and irreversible' and that this kind of attitude can impact on the ageing process. Social exclusion for older people can also be exacerbated when there are failures in service provision (Department of Work and Pensions 2006: 8).

The same report provides data which can be used as an indicator as to where old people might find themselves at more risk of social exclusion.

Now to the implications for social policy aspect of the question.

Research summary

From **Department of Work and Pensions** (2006)

The older people become, the more at risk they are from being excluded from basic service and social networks.

Ethnicity may be a factor as minority ethnic groups tend to experience higher levels of poverty, and generally there is a lower take-up of benefits among this age group.

The more deprived the area, the more likely older people living in this area might experience multiple dimensions of exclusion.

Where there is low household income there is a likelihood that older people will be excluded because they lack the resources to access services, social networks and cultural activities.

Griffin and Tyrrell (2003) postulate that when the following needs are met, an individual has a greater sense of engagement with life and their local community.

- Security, in terms of the community and dwelling.
- Financial resources to afford household utilities, food and recreational activities.
- Sense of autonomy and control over the decisions and choices made about life.
- Attention, that is being valued as a member of society.
- Emotional connection to others such as family and friends.
- Being part of a wider community through participation in interest groups; volunteering.
- Sense of status within social groupings.
- Sense of competence.
- Meaning and purpose.

Every dimension which might be lacking contributes to an older person feeling more excluded.

From this we can conclude that there are several aspects of social policy that are relevant to the quality of lives of older people. Income, housing and health are clearly of prime importance, and these are explored in more detail in the next two sections. Community involvement is also important, along with the practical arrangements that make that feasible, such as access to good public transport, systems of social networks, facilities for people to meet, and so on. All of this needs to be set in the context of the ability to make effective choices. Empowerment means being able to make one's own decisions, having an effective choice, being able to maintain independence for as long as possible. This does not necessarily imply increasing state involvement in people's lives, but does mean older people need to have information, access to information, and the power to make those decisions effective.

Poverty

Any discussion of poverty needs to acknowledge the definitional challenge. In a comparatively wealthy society such as Britain, poverty is relative in the sense that few people are completely lacking in any resources whatsoever. In this sense poverty means relative lack of wealth compared with other people. If you have studied sociology, you will doubtless be aware that there is a large literature on poverty, beginning with the seminal work of Townsend (1979). A recent research summary examines the whole issue of measuring poverty among older people and starts with the statement that the measurement of poverty is contested and complex and no measure really captures all the relevant elements (Price 2008: 1). It concludes by suggesting that poverty should be conceptualised as *having insufficient financial resources to participate in the norms and customs of society* and suggests that there are three options for measuring it: needs and deprivation; financial resources; and adequacy of financial resources according to individual needs (Price 2008: 8).

Research summary

Harrop and **Jopling** (2009) estimate that in Britain there are over 2 million old people living in poverty.

Sure Start to Later Life suggests that 20 per cent of pensioners were in relative poverty in 2003/04 and 16 per cent of pensioners are persistently poor (Department of Work and Pensions, 2006: 39).

We also need to take into account that poverty may have a differential impact. For example, ethnic minority pensioners are more likely to be in low-income households than white pensioners, and are also more likely to experience lack of central heating, car, telephone, and so on (**Department of Work and Pensions,** 2006: 38–39).

In terms of addressing the issue of poverty we may need to start by asking why differentials are tolerated. Here a longitudinal study commissioned by the Joseph Rowntree Foundation (Barber et al 2009) is pertinent. This revealed two specific attitudes that shed light on this. The first is the widespread notion that opportunities for success are readily available and that those who are wealthy 'deserve' to be so as they have taken advantage of these opportunities while the poor have not, and therefore by implication some older people are poor because they have failed to take advantage of opportunities earlier in their lives. The second underpinning belief discovered by the longitudinal study is 'fair inequality', meaning rich people were deserving of their wealth as they had taken on extra responsibilities, contributed to society in a way which benefited everyone while people on low incomes, especially those living on benefits, were considered to be unlikely to make a reciprocal contribution, and consequently do not deserve even the support they do actually receive (Barber et al. 2009: 3).

This may certainly help explain the somewhat grudging support offered to enhanced welfare benefits and pensions for older people. It may also help to explain why there is a comparatively poor take-up of some benefits – some older people simply believe they do not deserve them. This applies particularly to Income Guarantee, Housing Benefit and in particular Council Tax Benefit, with between 1.5 and 1.8 million pensioners not claiming (Department of Work and Pensions 2006: 39).

In addition to this factor, it may be that older people find the benefits and financial support system difficult to fathom. This relates not just to accessing the social security system but also to the financial arrangements connected to community care services. Here there are national criteria set down by the Department of Health called Fair Access to Care Services, yet, despite this set of rules, research by the King's Fund (2008) revealed that people with a similar level of disability still received different levels of entitlement ranging from fully funded care and accommodation for those who are assessed as meeting NHS continuing care criteria, through to nothing for those with assets of more than £21,500 who do not meet the NHS criteria (Caring Choice, 2008: 11). People who participated in the research also felt that the way in which the long-term care was funded varied among local authorities in terms of eligibility criteria and levels charged. There was a sense that rules regarding 'means-testing' of old peoples' financial situation was unfair and complex, so that an old person who had prepared for old age and had savings could become poor if they were to experience an extended period of disability.

Health and disability

The fifth point arising from our case study concerned health and disability. What is the evidence that older people have greater health needs than the rest of the population, and what health needs do they have? This information is essential as the basis on which health and social policies are to be formulated.

The annual Health Survey for England provides general statistical information, supplemented with occasional detailed reports. In 2005 the NHS Information Centre produced a special report on the care of older people (Craig and Mindell 2005).

Research summary

From **Craig** and **Mindell** (2005: 5)

Among both men and women aged 65 and over, 71 per cent reported longstanding illness; 42 per cent of men and 46 per cent of women reported that their illness limited their activities in some way. The prevalence of longstanding illness and limiting longstanding illness increased with age in both sexes. Limiting longstanding illness was higher among women than men aged 80–84 but was similar for other age groups.

The most commonly reported types of longstanding illness among both men and women aged 65 and over were musculoskeletal, and heart and circulatory diseases. In general, the rate of almost all of the conditions increased with age in both sexes.

Among people aged 65 and over, 37 per cent of men and 40 per cent of women reported having at least one functional limitation (seeing, hearing, communication, walking, or using stairs).

Prevalence of functional limitation increased with age, from 26 per cent of men and 25 per cent of women aged 65–69 to 57 per cent of men and 65 per cent of women aged 85 and over.

The number of functional limitations also increased with age: prevalence of reporting three or more limitations increased from 4 per cent of men and 2 per cent of women aged 65–69 to 17 per cent of men and 19 per cent of women aged 85 and over.

Men were more likely than women to have attended hospital as an outpatient in the past 12 months (53 per cent and 49 per cent respectively).

Outpatient attendance was more likely among older age groups: 15 per cent of both men and women had been admitted to hospital as inpatients in the preceding 12 months.

The likelihood of admission to hospital was again greater among older age groups, ranging from 10 per cent of men and women aged between 65 and 69 to 21 per cent of men aged between 75 and 79 and 21 per cent of women aged 85 or over.

So the general conclusion from this research is that health needs increase with age, perhaps not surprisingly. In addition, it looks as though health needs multiply as people get to their 80s. The social policy implications in terms of health provision in response to this are fairly straightforward, but there are some additional factors that need to be taken into account. For example:

- Are older people more likely to need help with some health conditions?
- Do particular groups of older people have greater health needs than others?

In answer to the first question, let's take two examples: sensory impairment and mental health.

The evidence that sensory impairments affect older people proportionally far more than the rest of the population is compelling.

Research summary

There are two million people with sight problems; 90 per cent are over age 60 (cited in Department of Work and Pensions 2006: 44).

A survey carried out for the RNIB suggests that only 47 per cent of old people have an eye test with the main barriers to the eye test being lack of own eye health awareness, cost of glasses, and transport problems (**Conway** and **McLaughlan**, 2005: 6).

The RNID cites the following figures: there are 8,945,000 deaf and hard-of-hearing people in the UK of whom 6,471,000 are aged over 60.

The RNID also provide more detailed information concerning over-70s: 71.1 per cent of over 70-year-olds will have some kind of hearing loss, 26.7 per cent mild hearing loss, 36.8 per cent moderate hearing loss, 6.3 per cent will have severe hearing loss, 1.3 per cent will have profound hearing loss (**RNID,** 2005 online).

The mental health of older people receives scant attention, particularly depression, which is an aspect of health of older people that is often overlooked.

Research summary

From **Craig** and **Mindell** (2005: 17–18)

It is estimated that nearly two-thirds of older people with a depressive illness have never discussed this with their GP.

Questions were included in the Health Survey for England in 2005 to assess the overall prevalence of depression among older people in the general population. This survey used the ten-item Geriatric Depression Scale which measured depressive symptoms such as feeling unhappy, feeling empty, helpless or hopeless. A score of three or more depressive symptoms was defined as a high score.

Women were more likely to have high scores than men (28 per cent and 22 per cent respectively), and high scores were more likely with increasing age among both sexes. The prevalence of high scores was 40 per cent for men aged 85 and over, compared with 19 per cent for men aged 65–69. For women, the proportion of those aged 85 and over with high scores was 43 per cent compared with 20 per cent of those aged 65–69.

The mental health voluntary organisation MIND published a document in 2005 entitled *MIND Exposes Severe Neglect of Older People*, which suggested that there are key concerns regarding the point at which services are no longer available for older people, and cite that this is normally around the age of 65 when the treatment choices available to older people becomes more restricted. They point out that once people attain the age of 65, availability of mental health services changes as people are then defined as an 'older person' rather than a 'working age adult'. This is reflected in funding criteria and results in age barriers in services. In addition, Mind claims that older people's mental health problems are often not recognised by doctors and hospital staff and they are seldom seen by psychiatrists. They quote statistics that suggest that only 6 per cent of people over the age of 75 are likely to be asked about suicide by their GP. One in six people develop clinical depression after they reach 65, 40 per cent of those in care homes. Dementia affects one in 20 people aged over 65 years, rising to one in five people over 80 (Mind 2005).

Netto (1998: 224) points out that depression is often associated with social isolation and poverty, yet addressing isolation and poverty can become more difficult when an old person has disabilities such as physical impairments. Harrop and Jopling (2009: 10) argue for careful future planning, and caution against underestimating the scale of the challenge *given the depths of poverty, isolation and disadvantage that so many older people face*. There needs to be the promotion of both physical and mental health as both prevention and early detection can have a significant impact on the aging experience. They conclude:

 public health strategies have not fully embraced the message 'never too early, never too late'.

Harrop and **Jopling** (2009: 38)

Turning now to the second question, and recalling earlier discussions in this chapter, it will be useful to focus on the specific needs that research has highlighted in relation to minority ethnic groups. Zahno and Rhule (2008: 18) point out that while the 2001 census data showed that nearly 50 per cent of people aged 65 and over were restricted by limiting long-term illness, the rates for Asian people were 60 per cent and black older people 54 per cent. They demonstrate that South Asian and black Caribbean old people are at an increased risk of specific diseases such as *diabetes, coronary heart disease, arthritis, stroke and respiratory disorders*. The higher susceptibility to these health conditions inevitably has an impact on the levels of disability which these people experience in old age. Yet there is a lower uptake in health and social care services despite research findings indicating that certain black and minority ethnic groups are at higher risk of certain health conditions. McIntosh (2008: 1) concludes that the health service often fails to identify the needs of black and minority ethnic older people, claiming that they are *not on the radar of the commissioning process* and what little data exists is not influencing strategic needs assessment for therapy, services or workforce planning.

It is clear from all of this is that there are certainly unmet health needs, but we can go further than this and say that, putting the discussion from this and the previous two sections together, it would be reasonable to conclude that in a variety of ways older people are socially excluded. The question is: can social policy address this? It is a question which you are now invited to answer.

Critical thinking exercise 5.7

How can social policy address the issue of social exclusion?

This would be a good assignment title. There are several aspects to this. Clearly poverty and health would need to be included, but you might also want to consider issues such as housing which we have not explored in this chapter.

Try to think of approaches that don't just rely on increasing state benefits. We have already highlighted a number of relevant issues such as lack of employment opportunities, low take-up of benefits, different healthcare needs. Can you think of strategies for addressing these?

This task is essentially for reflection and revision of what you have looked at so far in this chapter.

Older people as carers

The final aspect of the case study which we need to consider is another that is often overlooked, namely the role of older people as carers themselves, in particular their role in caring for each other and sometimes for older relatives, possibly even their own

---

parents. We are not here looking particularly at the general role of older people as carers of children, for example as grandparents, although that is certainly relevant if the children have special needs.

Research summary

From **Lloyd** (2009: 4–6)

Around 10 per cent of individuals aged 52 and above were providing some form of unpaid care in the year 2004.

Of these, 39 per cent cared for a spouse or partner, 11 per cent cared for an (adult) child with specific care needs, 34 per cent cared for their parent(s) or parent(s) in law, and 24 per cent for another category of person. However, individuals frequently care for more than one person.

The most important reason that older carers cite for the provision of care is that 'they are needed'. Significant minorities of older carers also cite feeling obliged, wanting to be useful and enjoyment as reasons for providing care.

Care provision varies by age, gender and the recipient of care. Women are consistently more likely than men to be carers, and the prevalence of unpaid care declines with age, except for spousal care, the prevalence of which increases with age.

Relatively few carers providing care to a parent or parent in law live with the person they care for. In contrast, most individuals providing care to a spouse or child do live with the person they care for.

Providers of parental care typically provide far fewer hours of care per week than other types of older carer. Among older carers of spouses and adult children, the situation is reversed: care provision is clearly skewed toward 'heavy care'.

Spousal carers are typically older, poorer, provide a larger volume of care and experience poorer outcomes than, for example, older carers providing care for a parent.

Older carers providing moderate to heavy volumes of care (20+ hours per week) report a significantly lower quality of life than comparable non-carers.

Comparing the lives of carers and non-carers, it was found that providers of moderate to heavy care have more difficulty accessing health services and local shops.

Older carers are more likely than non-carers to wish that they could go to the cinema more often, suggesting that caring responsibilities do constrain aspirations to participate in leisure activities. Spousal carers are less likely to have holidayed in the UK or abroad than non-carers.

The role that carers generally play in supporting older people is now more widely recognised, although it has taken some time for this to be translated into separate rights for carers, in the form of legislation such as the Carers (Equal Opportunities) Act 2004. It is now specifically addressed in government policy documents which acknowledge the increased demands that will inevitably be placed on carers because of demographic trends (Department of Health 2008: 32). Harrop and Jopling (2009: 33) estimate that unpaid carers provide the equivalent of £87 billion a year in care and support. They also point out that changing patterns of family life, combined with increasing pressures to work longer, may reduce the potential supply of informal care from adult offspring. This is a particular issue for gay and lesbian older people. Consequently, they say, there is increasing pressure on one partner to become the carer for the other. There is a limitation of current provision in that, while carers have a right to be assessed, they do not necessarily have the right to receive help that they need. Furthermore, when carers do receive support, often the main purpose is to bolster them in their caring role rather than the focus being on their own quality of life.

Netto (1998: 223) offers a case vignette of a woman from an ethnic minority group in her sixties who has numerous health issues, has high blood pressure, undergone three eye operations and is a carer for her husband. *I forget myself,* she says, *because I have to look after him every minute, every second.* Changes in attitudes towards caring need to be taken into account, both over time and between cultures. For example, a carer who has grown up in the United Kingdom and who now looks after her mother-in-law who resided in Hong Kong stated *Her being old, with different values and living in the same house. We try to avoid clashes* (Netto 1998: 223). Service provision needs to be sensitive to these generational shifts within ethnic groups and aware of potential conflicts which may arise due to intergenerational differences.

Some care elements can be particularly challenging for older carers. Netto (1998: 224) suggests that these challenges often relate to bathing, dressing and physical help in walking; this at a time when the carer themselves may not be as physically fit as they once were. Both these factors need to be taken into account when devising care policies. A proactive approach needs to be taken in the service provision for ethnic minority groups, and services need to take into consideration the cultural isolation which can be experienced (Netto 1998: 225).

Returning to theories

In Chapter 2 you were introduced to liberalism, which returned in its updated neo-liberalist New Right format in the 1980s by promoting individual freedom and 'rolling back the frontiers of the state', as explained in Chapter 4. Chapter 3 summarised a different approach which emphasised social democratic views connected to citizenship and positive freedom, promoting state intervention to enhance people's well-being. This also influenced more recent New Labour policies. We are now going to explore how these might relate to the six areas explored in this chapter which emerged from the analysis of the case study.

Critical thinking exercise 5.8

How would social policy based on liberalist views address the aspects of older people's lives explored in this chapter? Compare and contrast these to social policy based on social democratic ideas.

The aspects are:

- diversity;
- age discrimination;
- social exclusion;
- poverty;
- health and disability;
- older carers.

You will find one suggestion as to how to tackle this comparison at the end of this book, together with some suggested responses that each approach might make.

Chapter Summary

In this chapter we used a case study to explore the lived reality of older people's lives in Britain, drawing out from this elements that need to be considered when thinking about social policy. The analysis included reference to a fair amount of demographic material, which was related to the increasing diversity of the older age group, and to the general challenge of the ageing population. The discussion covered age discrimination, and then the potential for older people to be socially excluded, either through lack of social contact or else through loss of income, or loss of health and general well-being. Finally, attention was drawn to the fact that many older people are carers themselves, and not just the recipients of care services.

In terms of skills development, it is hoped that you will be now be familiar with the challenge of interpreting some elementary statistical data that was primarily drawn from census material. Considerable emphasis was placed on exploring ways in which social policy can address the specific needs highlighted in this chapter. Much of this centred on you thinking of the implications for policy, and at the end of the chapter this was related back to the theory discussed in the early part of the book. Hopefully you will now be able to see that there are clear differences of approach to social policy with older people, and you may want to spend time thinking about the implications of this for social work practice. In the next chapter, this theme is taken up by an exposition of some contemporary social policy initiatives that are brought together under the heading of personalisation.

This is beginning to have a profound impact on social work practice, as you will see.

Further reading

British Journal of Social Work (2007) Special Issue on Adult Care, vol. 37 (3).
Contains a number of relevant articles on adult care, primarily from a social work practice perspective, but with many cross-references to social policy.

Office of National Statistics (2010) *Social Trends.* Available at **www.statistics.gov.uk.**
The national repository for data includes analysis of a huge range of official statistics relating to topics of relevance to social policy and social work. Also provides access to census data and a number of explanatory comments and reports on that data.

Lymbery, M. (2005) *Social Work with Older People: Context, Policy and Practice.* London: Sage.
Includes good chapters on social policy context and offers a thoughtful overview of work in this area.

HM Government (2008) *Carers at the Heart of 21st-Century Families.* London: Department of Health.
Summary of current policy relating to carers.

HM Government (2007) *Putting People First.* London: Department of Health.
Summary of current policy relating to adult care generally. There will be more on this in the next chapter.

6

Older People, Social Policy and Empowerment:
More Choice, More Say?

Nicolette Wade and Robert Johns

Achieving a Social Work or Social Policy Degree

Exercises in this chapter will focus on

- ⊙ skill 4   evaluating different perspectives and ideas
- ⊙ skill 6   synthesising arguments
- ⊙ skill 8   reviewing, re-evaluating and reformulating your own views

This chapter is relevant to a number of Social Policy Benchmarks.

3.2   main features of the interrelationship between social policies and differently placed communities, families and individuals

3.3   history of contemporary social problems and of social policy responses to them

Its content is also of particular relevance to the following Social Work Subject Benchmarks.

5.1.2 the complex relationships between public, social and political philosophies, policies and priorities and the organisation and practice of social work issues and trends in modern public and social policy and their relationship to contemporary practice and service delivery in social work the significance of legislative and legal frameworks and service delivery standards the development of personalised services, individual budgets and direct payments

---

Introduction

Chapters 2–4 of this book introduced you to the idea that political ideology shapes and influences social policy. In particular you were asked to think about how the relationship between the state and the individual has been seen at various points. Over the course of the last two centuries we have seen significant changes in how that relationship has been viewed and in turn translated into social policy. At the heart of the matter are questions of individual and collective responsibility: how much should people be responsible for their own well-being and how much of a role should the state play in providing for people?

The start of the last century saw the introduction of old age pensions and at roughly the mid-century stage the welfare state was created. The 1980s New Right withdrawal from ideas of collective responsibility promoted individual responsibility with the introduction of markets into the social and healthcare arena. The last decade of the twentieth century, under New Labour, was marked by a continuation of these policies coupled with increased central control and regulation in an effort to improve quality and safeguards. The first decade of the twenty-first century saw a new policy direction described as 'transforming' adult social care (HM Government 2007). The key term attached to this new direction is 'personalisation', linked to empowerment and choice, for reasons which will become clear as this chapter unfolds.

Personalisation represents a move towards service users taking greater responsibility for choosing and securing services themselves. Questions that arise centre on how this should result in greater empowerment for older people. Fundamental to such a social policy analysis is an exploration of what lies behind these developments.

In order to undertake this quest, let's start as usual with a case study.

CASE STUDY

Grace Lewis is 75 years old, divorced and lives alone in a small terraced house which she owns and has lived in for the last 30 years. The property is run down and in need of modernisation and repair. Grace has two children, Tina aged 50 who lives over 100 miles away and Sandra aged 48 who lives in the same town as her mother. Both daughters work full time and are single parents, each being the mother of two teenage children. Grace does not have an occupational pension and relies on the state pension as her only means of financial support. In recent years Grace's physical health has been deteriorating, she has arthritis and has become depressed and socially isolated. Her ability to manage the tasks associated with daily living such as washing, preparing meals, looking after her home and shopping are becoming increasingly difficult for her.

The case study will be used throughout this chapter to illustrate what personalisation is, how it might work and what the potential impacts of personalisation may be. However, we need to start by asking the preliminary question which connects this case study to the discussion in Chapter 5: why might it be necessary to 'transform' adult social care?

Critical thinking exercise 6.1

Why do you think it has become necessary to change policy and 'transform' adult social care?

If you have difficulties answering this question, it will repay you to look back at Chapter 5. You might also want to look back at the earlier discussion in Chapters 3 and 4 about social democratic principles, for remember that these generally underpin the thinking of Labour governments. Some suggested answers now follow.

1. Demographic trends: increasing numbers of older people mean an increase in demand for services, which services would have to accommodate. This necessarily means looking again at the way services are organised and delivered. This aspect was covered in detail in Chapter 5. For a quick overview of the way in which demand for community care services are expected to rise up to 2026, take a look at Table 6.1, remembering that the figures are in billions.

Table 6.1: Costs to state and individuals of current means-testing system (2006/7 prices, £billion)

	Costs to service users themselves	Costs to public	Total costs of care services
2010	6.9	6.4	13.3
2011	7.0	6.7	13.7
2012	7.3	7.1	14.4
2013	7.7	7.4	15.1
2014	8.1	7.7	15.8
2015	8.2	8.1	16.3
2020	10.5	9.7	20.2
2025	13.1	11.7	24.8

Humphries et al. (2010: 46)

2. For reasons explained in Chapter 5, an increase in the proportion of older people without a commensurate increase in people of working age necessarily means that services will cost proportionately more, and so the most efficient way of delivering services needs to be devised. Services could be curtailed of course, and access to the most expensive services severely limited. You will recall from Chapter 3 that residential care appeared to be used in cases where we would now argue that community services would be much more suitable. Not only would they be more appropriate, but they would also be cheaper, so services may have had to change to encourage yet more use of community services.

3. Furthermore, recent financial crises in the global economy will result in severe constraints on public expenditure. This means that services cannot just be expanded on the current model, but services may need to be reconfigured. In addition it may be necessary for access to services to be controlled through some kind of rationing system, either imposed through the needs assessment process, or else ideologically created through expectations that people will make their own provision rather than rely on the state.

4. Moving away from economic and financial considerations, there have also been social changes that affect the lives of older people, which consequently may mean they need different kinds of services. We looked at a number of these issues in Chapter 5: diversity, poverty, health and disability, social isolation. There are elements of all of these in the case study. In a highly diverse society, services need to be correspondingly diverse and geared to the needs of a wide range of people.
5. Strongly associated with this is what might be called the social dignity aspect, which also connects to both social democratic and neo-liberalist principles. Again we touched on this in Chapter 5. If people are to be respected as citizens, they need to be included in decisions over their lives. They need to feel that they have choice over what services are provided; they should not be made to feel that they are the recipients of some kind of charity. Although neo-liberalism seems diametrically opposed to social democratic thinking, here they would converge because neo-liberalism argues that people should be free as much as possible from state intervention. So giving people freedom to choose services means that the state does not decide for them, and therefore the state does not impinge on their lives quite to the same extent.
6. This trend is reinforced by the growth in the service user movement, which has meant that people have come together to articulate more clearly and emphatically that they want services that are responsive to individual needs, and over which they have some control, usually through participation in management and quality-assurance processes.

There are also some reasons, of which you may well be unaware, connected to the way in which local authorities are currently organised in order to provide community care services for older people.

> At present, the purchasing of many public services is done through local authority commissioners who buy what a local authority area needs in terms of health or social care for two or three years at a time. Although this brings large economies of scale, the resulting inflexibility turns out to be expensive. When local authorities buy services in blocks, much of the money tends to go on expensive institutional care like residential homes, and this often traps people in a cycle of dependency or isolation, with little or no say over what they receive. This leads to 'Parkinson's Law': that demand will always increase to match supply.
>
> **Bartlett** (2009: 15)

So there is a problem arising from the current commissioning arrangements which derive from the implementation of the National Health Service and Community Care Act 1990. Bartlett also argues that if efficiencies are to be made using this model of provision, the scope is limited. For example, the local authority could raise the criteria for eligibility. In essence this is what has happened over recent years and now most authorities have set eligibility at the critical or substantial level. The general trend has been for fewer people to receive a higher level of support (Alcock et al. 2008). The other option is to try to drive down the cost, but again there is a limit to this, since those working in the home care and residential sectors are among the least well paid. So instead Bartlett focuses on the inefficiencies in the current system and highlights the issue of putting people into services which are already available, which may not necessarily be the most efficient or effective way of meeting their needs. Similarly with home care provision; it is limited, if publically funded, to personal care only. The argument put forward is that the eligible person may actually need help with domestic work because personal care needs can be met by a family member, but all that is available is the more expensive personal care.

If you found it difficult to grasp some of these arguments, do not worry, for they will be revisited during the course of this chapter.

This chapter explores the transformation of adult care services and the development of personalisation for older people in the first decade of the twenty-first century. The chapter title echoes the emphasis in the various Green and White Papers published since 2005 which have promoted choice, independence and a particular version of empowerment.

The first part of the chapter considers what exactly is meant by transformation and personalisation, following on from the explanations of the need for change itemised above. Included in this will be a summary of the key changes of approach, with references to the most significant policy documents, all of which say something about the relationship between the state and older people in terms of the role of the individual and the community, the role of the state, and mutual responsibilities. Also included here will be some discussion of conclusions that can be drawn from research evidence.

The second part of the chapter will focus on implementation, not in a general sense but in relation to the case study above. Here there will be an attempt to explain how personalisation might apply in various permutations, using this basic scenario. The discussion here will of course be in a policy context; it is outside the remit of this book to explore the full range of needs that Grace and Tina may have.

In the third section the focus turns to the current physical and economic context, and explores some examples of the types of initiatives that are being developed in response to the transformation and personalisation agenda. In other words, it looks at how ideas and ideals become translated into actual services delivered to real people, but also in the likely real context of an increase in the older population and constrained public expenditure.

The final section turns its focus to social work practice, focusing on the role of social work in this new terrain. It should be noted, though, that the implementation of the policy is at different stages throughout the country. Some local authorities are further along the road than others, so this chapter is rather different from other chapters in the book insofar as it is referring to new social policy in the early stages of development.

The transformation of adult care services: Personalisation

Having explored some explanations as to why it was necessary to 'transform' adult social care – and of course you may have thought of others for yourself not listed above – we now need to explain what form those changes have taken. In a nutshell, the major transformation is 'personalisation'.

Personalisation, naturally, involves people making personal choices. The idea of extending choice to adult social care users, including older people, is not in fact new. The policy underpinning the introduction of the National Health Service and Community Care Act 1990 was promoted in terms of improving choice through the introduction of a market based on a mixed economy of social care providers, although there were other reasons for this policy, as we saw in Chapter 4. One of the key points to be explored in this chapter is to consider what is meant by choice in the context of personalisation and how choice is being extended. Moving this towards the future, we might ask what is going to be different as a result of recent proposals and initiatives: are they likely to result in wider choice, more personalised services, and ultimately greater empowerment for older people?

Both the Adult Social Care Green Paper entitled *Independence, Well-being and Choice* (Department of Health, 2005b) and the subsequent White Paper entitled *Our Health, Our Care, Our Say: A New Direction for Community Services* (Department of Health 2006) promote the concept of service user choice. An important point to note, in passing, is that personalisation is directed at all adult users of social care; it is not a policy aim directed specifically at older people alone. Another point worth noting here is the difference between Green Papers and White Papers: Green Papers are declarations from government that they are planning some policy changes by setting out some possibilities and inviting comments; a White Paper is a clear statement of intended government policy, which may then subsequently be debated by Parliament and translated into legislation.

Critical thinking exercise 6.2

This is a pause for thought. You might want to reflect on the language used in the titles of policy documents, and of course in the documents themselves. From a sociological point of view, language is important as it sets the context and parameters of debate. You might note the consistently upbeat terminology used in many of the policy documents, some of which may have a particular downbeat or chilling message.

This is intended just as a reflection exercise, but there is another interesting example coming up immediately.

Following on from the White Paper, the government issued a 'ministerial concordat', *Putting People First: A Shared Vision and Commitment to the Transformation of Adult Social Care* (HM Government 2007), based on an interdepartmental agreement as to how the new adult care policy was to be implemented. This set the direction for adult social care over the next ten years and more, referring to the 'transformation' of adult social care being based on principles of:

- a commitment to independent living;
- collaboration across all relevant bodies;
- reform which is co-produced, co-developed and co-evaluated with service users;
- meaningful change is linked to empowering service users;
- winning the hearts and minds of staff;
- a shift from paternalistic reactive care to prevention and high-quality tailored services;
- the role of statutory agencies to be more enabling and less controlling;
- a greater emphasis on self-assessment;
- social workers spending more time on support, brokerage and advocacy;
- personal budgets.

As one might expect, with any policy transformation, there are a number of new terms associated with it. Below is a brief summary of the key terms which may be unfamiliar to you. These have been adapted from *Personalisation: A Rough Guide* (SCIE 2010).

Personalisation

Personalisation means thinking about care and support services in an entirely different way. This means starting with the person as an individual with strengths, preferences and aspirations and putting them at the centre of the process of identifying their needs and making choices about how and when they are supported to live their lives. It requires a significant transformation of adult social care so that all systems, processes, staff and services are geared up to put people first.

SCIE (2010: 3)

Self-directed support
Self-directed support relates to a variety of approaches to creating personalised social care and is seen as the route to achieving independent living.

> The defining characteristics of self-directed support are:
>
> the support is controlled by the individual
>
> the level of support is agreed in a fair, open and flexible way
>
> any additional help needed to plan, specify and find support should be provided by people who are as close to the individual as possible
>
> the individual should control the financial resources for their support in a way they choose
>
> all of the practices should be carried out in accordance with an agreed set of ethical principles.
>
> **SCIE** (2010: 5–6)

Individual or personal budgets

An individual budget is an overall budget for a range of services, not just from social care, and could include cash or services or a mixture of both. The term 'personal budget' has been used interchangeably with 'individual budget', although more recently some commentators have assumed that personal budget applies only to the use of social care resources whereas an individual budget relates to a budget which is derived from a wider range of sources.

The Care Quality Commission reported in February 2010 that 115,000 adults over 18 in England were receiving a personal budget or direct payment option, which represents 6.5 per cent of all adults using services in 2008/9, but just 3.6 per cent of people over 65 (Care Quality Commission 2010: 30).

Resource allocation system

Resource allocation systems are ways of determining the size of personal or individual budgets. The intention is to itemise the levels of help a user requires across a number of domains in order to achieve particular outcomes; each answer is scored reflecting the level of need, and the individual score is then translated into a single sum of money. The intention is that this sum of money is made known to the service user at an early stage in the process so that the individual can then develop an individual support plan. There is national variation in relation to both interpretation and implementation of resource allocation systems (ADASS/DoH 2009).

Within the resource allocation system, the term 'funding streams' refers to the range of different sources which could make up an individual budget. These include local authority adult social care, community equipment services, Disabled Facilities Grants, housing-related support, access to work and Independent Living Fund. However, not all of these funding sources are available to older people.

Direct payments

A direct payment:

is a means-tested cash payment made in the place of regular social service provision to an individual who has been assessed as needing support. Following a financial assessment, those eligible can choose to take a direct payment and arrange for their own support instead. The money included in a direct payment only applies to social services ... As part of self-directed support, the personal budget holder is encouraged to devise a support plan to help them meet their personal outcomes ... Once a plan has been devised support can be purchased from: statutory social services, the private sector, the voluntary or third sector, user-led organisations, community groups, neighbours, family and friends.

SCIE (2010: 10–11)

Direct payments were introduced by the Community Care (Direct Payments) Act 1996 for younger adults and their availability was extended to older people in 2000. In 2001 it became a duty for local authorities to offer direct payments to eligible people. In relation to the overall number of adults receiving services, the number of people receiving direct payments is relatively small. For example, in 2008–9 services were received by 1,216,000 people aged 65 or over, of whom 1,016,000 received community services. Of these, only 37,000 received direct payments, although direct payments are increasing at a faster rate for clients aged 65 and over (36 per cent increase from 2007–08) compared with younger adults (24 per cent increase) (Health and Social Care Information Centre 2010). This suggests that the logistics of transformation constitutes a fairly formidable challenge.

Policy in practice: Examining the research

Critical thinking exercise 6.3

Why do you think the number of older people receiving direct payments is small in comparison to the total number of people aged over 65 assessed as being eligible for services?

Is this evidence of ageism? What are the social policy implications ?

Ellis (2007) has undertaken some research into the question of comparatively poor take-up of direct payments and has highlighted a range of issues which have compromised the expansion of direct payments. These issues included:

- low staff awareness of direct payments and lack of confidence in using them;
- paternalistic approaches to risk;
- cumbersome and time-consuming systems for operating direct payments;
- being seen as inappropriate by social workers in situations of crisis or in situations characterised by high levels of dependency;
- conflict with the role of supporting carers;
- organisational ambiguity about the use of direct payments;
- social workers perceiving older people as being vulnerable and in need of care;
- distinctions being made between deserving and undeserving recipients;
- linking assessments of the level of independence to the ability to manage direct payments rather than seeing direct payments as a means to achieving independence;
- social workers seeing direct payments as a threat to their role and decision-making powers.

These research findings coupled with the facts about take-up of direct payments suggest that social workers and their employing local authorities have not been entirely supportive of direct payments, particularly for older people. While there may be sound social work reasons in individual cases for this apparent lack of enthusiasm, the focus of this book is on social policy so we need to consider some of the challenges of translating policy into practice here.

One inference that could be drawn from this is that social policy implementation has not been sufficiently robust in order to achieve the aim of extending direct payments to all who are eligible. However, regulations exist that virtually require it. In England the relevant law is the Community Care, Services for Carers and Children's Services (Direct Payments) (England) Regulations 2003 (Statutory Instrument 2003 No. 762) which places a duty on local authorities to offer a direct payment to an adult if the responsible authority is satisfied that the person's needs for services can be met by securing the provision of them by means of a direct payment. Given the data already cited from the Health and Social Care Information Centre, it suggests that the duty to offer a direct payment has not been sufficient in itself to expand the level of take-up which the government would like to see.

It may also be the case that a direct payment may not offer the means to meet the identified need. Why might this be the case? Possible reasons, in addition to those posed by Ellis (2007), include seeing how previous or historic social policy has shaped cultural expectations on the part of social workers, older people themselves and their families. It is when we start to appreciate how the past has shaped the current situation, that we start to get some sense of what 'transformation' might mean. In this context, namely the provision of services to eligible older people, we get some sense that 'transformation' is to do with changing the expectation that older people will be cared for by the state to a new culture based on the premise that older people will be given the means to look after themselves.

Is this evidence of ageism? As we saw in Chapter 1, there is some debate as to what constitutes ageism. It is certainly not just examples of individual prejudice, for ageism covers a whole spectrum ranging from institutional discrimination including legal discrimination, internalised ageism (having a negative personal view of older people) through to benevolent patronage marked by sayings such as 'poor old dear'.

There are number of reasons why we might suggest that the research findings do indeed indicate evidence of ageism. It may be that social workers are making judgements about older people resulting in the view that they are vulnerable and in need of care, suggesting passivity and dependence, thus constraining any potential for independence. Furthermore, the evidence presented suggests that this may be linked to paternalistic attitudes held by social workers feeling fearful about a loss of power, status and role.

An alternative explanation may be found in highlighting the considerations which we looked at in Chapter 5, such as:

- the connection between needing services and poverty;
- the relationship between relative deprivation over the course of a lifetime and need in old age;
- at a time of crisis brought on by ill health or isolation, or both factors together, do older people want to direct their own care?

Above all it must be remembered that while older people will share some characteristics, as we saw in Chapter 5, they also comprise a diverse group marked by differences in life experience, opportunity, expectations, health, ability and resources, to name but some of the features which denote us all as individuals. Even so, given that personalisation encompasses person-centred planning and person-centred care, this ought to reflect a recognition that people are individuals and that services should be shaped around them rather than people fitting into services. As such there is a strong link to the value base which underpins social work so perhaps it is surprising that the take-up has been comparatively low.

This is especially true if we return to the principles underpinning personalisation, so now we consider the social policy implications. Earlier we indicated that personalisation is consistent with the idea of promoting service users as citizens, as equal to professionals making assessments and judgements, able to challenge and deliberate with them. Furthermore, service users are not to be regarded as mere consumers, choosing between different packages offered to them. In this way, personalisation seeks to overcome the limitations of both paternalism and consumerism. Some people have criticised the care management system established in the 1990s as having both these features. A central theme of the work of Leadbetter (2004), one of the influential proponents of personalisation, is the idea that service users are seen as the co-designers and co-producers of the goods in question. The vision is that society has huge untapped resources and that the role of public service professionals is to help create environments which allow people in need of services to devise solutions in radical ways. Leadbetter argues that the real challenge is *how do we create more personalised public services to help people to devise their own, bottom up solutions, which create the public good?* (Leadbetter 2004: 26). The public good is linked to the idea that wider social benefits would exist from such an approach, particularly efficiency. Efficiency, he argues, comes from solving problems rather than managing them and getting things right the first time. He suggests that reforms should take the following direction.

- *Promote new sources of information for users.*
- *Create new interfaces such as NHS Direct allowing access to advice and services.*
- *Provide professionals with the skills and support to become brokers and advisors as well as solution providers.*
- *Change funding regimes to give users more influence over how the money is spent.*
- *Give service users a right to a voice in the design of the services they use.*

Leadbetter (2004: 96)

Implementing personalisation: Applying policy to the case study

Let us return to Grace and consider what personalisation might mean for her and her daughters in light of a range of scenarios.

Scenario 1

Sandra, Grace's daughter and main carer, has been offered a new job which requires her to relocate to a town 50 miles away from where she currently lives. The job is a significant promotion and will help secure Sandra's financial future.

Scenario 2

Grace has a fall at home and as a result fractures her wrist. It is not necessary for her to remain in hospital and at the same time she is unable to look after herself. The fall has shaken her confidence and she feels very anxious about being alone.

Scenario 3

Sandra is becoming very concerned about Grace. She has noticed that her mother is losing weight, is becoming quite forgetful and seems disorientated. Sandra thinks that Grace cannot safely be left on her own. Grace is visibly distressed when Sandra leaves her after calling each day.

Each of the above scenarios represents some change to the situation you were presented with at the beginning of the chapter and seem to indicate that action is required by someone in order to promote Grace's welfare. Under the care management process, assessment would be the cornerstone of any intervention. Provided that Grace satisfies the eligibility criteria under Fair Access to Care Services or equivalent, a social worker would complete the assessment with Grace and Sandra and discuss the ways in which identified needs could be met (Fair Access to Care Services is the Department of Health guidance on who is eligible for community care services in England, which categorises needs into four headings: critical, substantial, moderate and low).

One of the key themes outlined in the personalisation agenda is a greater emphasis on self-assessment.

Research summary

The Association of Directors of Adult Social Services and the Local Government Association surveyed all 150 English local authorities about progress in implementing Putting People First in 2008/9, the first year of the programme. Of these, 141 authorities were considering significant changes to assessment and care management arrangements, affecting the majority of care management staff. About half of respondents stated that it would affect all assessment and care management staff and about a further half a significant proportion of them. 80 authorities reported that they currently operated supported self-assessment; 18 of these already have this in place for most people, and a further 62 for some. The remainder intended to have supported self assessment operating within the next 12 months. 122 local authorities reported that the resource allocation systems that are in place or are proposed will be points based.

Source: **ADASS/LGA** (2009: 3–4)

The In Control report states that older people were more likely to report improvements in their quality of life if a social worker had supported them in their personal support planning.

Source: **Glendinning** (2008)

We can see from the above that change is afoot on various levels and that over the course of the next few years that rate of change is likely to escalate. The changes relate to introducing new ways of identifying need based on self-assessment and that a self-assessment will result in points being awarded, which in turn will relate to offering individuals the means to develop a personal support plan linked to a personal budget.

The three scenarios suggest varying levels of urgency about the situation; however, the policy of personalisation clearly puts the onus on Grace to identify her own needs and work out how they can best be met. Evidence from the In Control report and the other individual budget pilot studies suggest that the outcomes for older people are better if they are supported in these activities (Glendinning 2008; Ellis 2007). Again, the emphasis in the personalisation agenda is on family and friends being the main source of that support.

Critical thinking exercise 6.4

Will this empower Grace?

What are the merits of personalisation here? What might be its shortcomings as far as she is concerned?

This is a question that invites you to reflect on how policy impinges on practice and vice versa. A discussion of this follows, so now is the opportunity to take time out to reflect on this question.

Looking at scenario 1, a number of tensions become evident. If Sandra is to take up her new job it will mean that she moves and will not be in a position to provide the daily support currently offered to her mother. Personalisation offers the opportunity for her to support Grace in producing a self-assessment. How will this be done? Clearly, having easy access to understandable and good-quality information about how to complete a self-assessment will be important, as will the ease of completing any document.

The other significant aspect is how Grace and Sandra will work out the best way of meeting those needs. Again, having access to information about a range of service options will be crucial to promoting choice. Who will provide this information? Even if Grace and Sandra have a good idea of how needs could be met, how will they know if this is the best or only way of meeting those needs? The wider issue associated with this scenario is the tension for Sandra, as a divorced woman who is also a carer.

On the one hand, personalisation is concerned with the maintenance of independence and choice. If Sandra takes up the job she will potentially help secure her own future by having greater financial stability and thus in her old age stands a greater probability of maintaining independence; she will also in the meantime be increasing her tax contribution, which helps to pay for community care services for older people. So in social policy terms this might be a good option. If, however, she remains where she is in order to provide support to Grace, she runs the risk of compromising her own well-being both in the short and long term. The pressures faced by carers of older people has been widely documented (see for example Bernard 2007) and there is specific policy guidance that addresses this (Department of Health 2008, 1999). Furthermore, we might ask if Sandra's choice is being restricted by a policy which puts too great an emphasis on individuals being supported by relatives. Again, looking ahead, who would support Grace after Sandra has moved away if the support plan did not work out as intended?

On the other hand, potentially personalisation offers the opportunity for an outcome to be tailor-made and responsive to the individual. This may afford the opportunity to develop a plan which offers something better than the services which have traditionally been available. For example, a personal assistant – perhaps someone who is already known to and trusted by the family – could be employed. Later in the chapter we will look at some of the initiatives which have been developed to support the personalisation agenda. However, of the three scenarios this is the least urgent.

Scenario 2 is about a sudden change which tips a situation which was manageable into one which, at least temporarily, is not. Questions which this scenario raises are to do with the capacity of a policy which primarily hinges around the ability of people to manage their own affairs (with or without support) in a situation of sudden change. *Putting People First* (HM Government 2007) makes the point that with the freedom to direct one's own care also comes the responsibility. Who is responsible in this scenario? Again, we can imagine that Sandra will be integral to whatever arrangements are made. If Grace did not have any relatives, who would support her with making the necessary arrangements to maintain her independence? Given the psychological impact of the fall on Grace, does she actually want to be alone at this time? On the other hand, do the sorts of initiatives which are being developed as a result of the personalisation agenda provide scope for new forms of support which allow greater dignity and independence? Further detail is provided later on in the chapter about these initiatives.

Scenario 3 refers to a situation of a more gradual rise in the level of apparent need. The change which Sandra has noted may stem from the social isolation experienced by Grace which has led to her depression worsening; if you recall, social isolation and depression were discussed in general terms in Chapter 5. Prevention is a key element of personalisation. The fundamental question that this raises is: would the development of low-level, community-based services designed to promote social inclusion prevent Grace's depression and thus enable her to maintain maximum independence for a longer period?

At the heart of Grace's situation and the policy response to it is the question of funding. Resources are finite and social policy, as has been noted earlier in this and previous chapters, is very much concerned with how the balance of responsibility between the state and the individual is worked out. The debate about funding the care of older people is not a new one. Various bodies including the Royal Commission on the Funding of Long Term Care (Sutherland 1999) concluded that current funding arrangements were inadequate. The government, however, rejected the proposal from the Royal Commission that long-term care, whether social or health, should be paid for out of general taxation, although subsequently following the creation of the Scottish Parliament this policy was implemented in Scotland. Instead in England and Wales the government agreed to nursing care being paid for from taxation. Personal care, which includes bathing, feeding and dressing, remained social care and subject to means-testing and eligibility criteria, thus controlling costs.

Hirsch (2005) argues in a paper for the Joseph Rowntree Foundation that current arrangements fall short in three main ways.

> - In overall funding levels. There are already signs that needs are going unmet. Without change, private individuals will have to foot a growing share of rising costs, and many will find this hard to afford.
> - In coherence. Multiple funding streams create confusing and sometimes irrational, overlapping ways of paying for care.
> - In fairness, in terms of the way costs and responsibilities are shared. Family carers often feel unsupported. Means-testing causes widespread resentment by taking away most of people's assets and income before they can get state help.

An element in the case study not touched upon so far is the position of Tina relative to Sandra. Tina, living some distance away, is not able to support her mother as Sandra does. Grace's only financial asset is her house. If it became necessary for Grace to move into residential care on a permanent basis, proceeds from the house sale would be used to fund that care because the state does not fund personal care if a person has assets above a certain level. If Grace remains in her home, the outcome of a means test would be based on her income, which is derived from benefits. This is likely to result in a minimal or no contribution to the cost of a support package and would not entail the house being sold. This situation has a number of potential implications which will now be considered.

Critical thinking exercise 6.5

- How might these arrangements influence Sandra and Tina?
- If Sandra continues to support her mother, should this be reflected in any future inheritance after the house has been sold?
- Are these issues private or public matters?

It is possible that considerations relating to future financial gain through inheritance may influence all the family members including Grace. For example, it might be more important to Grace to leave her daughters an inheritance rather than fund her care. It is also possible that Sandra and Tina may put their own interests before their mother's in deciding what to do. This raises potential safeguarding issues. Some commentators have expressed concern that personalisation may make older people more vulnerable to abuse or exploitation by others (Manthorpe et al. 2009).

Many people might consider it would be fair if Sandra's support of her mother was reflected in a future inheritance; others might say Tina would help if she could and therefore should not be penalised. Legally, it is entirely up to Grace as to how she chooses to leave her assets and is therefore in essence a private matter. However, personalisation as a policy does place expectations on private individuals who are family members – namely that they are the first point of call if a person needs support. The evidence suggests that older people are more likely to own a house compared with younger adults in need of services, which in turn raises questions about the distribution of assets in relation to a supporting or caring role. At this time the public debate is focused largely on whether people should fund their own care or not. It has yet to move into the territory of considering what, if any, role the state may have in determining how resources may be used in this wider sense.

The discussion now moves to a wider context, yet still focusing on how social policy affects individuals, such as those in our case study.

Research summary: Individual budgets

The Care Quality Commission, the independent regulator for health and adult social care services, reported in 2009 that a third of councils must improve their ability to care for people with dignity and respect (Care Quality Commission 2009). Specifically a quarter of councils have been rated as only adequate when providing people with choice and control over their care, which suggests that only limited opportunities were being offered to participate in the Individual Budget Pilot Programme.

In 2005, 13 representative local authorities were selected for a programme run by the Department of Health that created pilot sites to facilitate a policy evaluation of individual budgets, the Individual Budget Pilot Programme. The evaluation team comprised of researchers from five universities and covered a period from November 2005 until December 2007. The aims of the evaluation were to examine whether individual budgets offered a better way of supporting people with social care needs than conventional methods, examine the relative merits of individual budgets for different groups of people and to explore the impacts of individual budgets on the workforce. Across the 13 pilot sites, 959 people were included in the sample; of these 510 were in the individual budget group and 449 were in the comparison group. An essential part of the research was to compare outcomes for these two groups. Within this, 28 per cent or 263 were older people, the other groups included working-age physically disabled (34 per cent), people with learning disabilities (25 per cent) and those who used mental health services of working age (14 per cent).

The following is an extract from the final report assessing the evidence in relation to older people.

The results of the evaluation also raise questions about the benefits of Individual Budgets for older people and how these can be maximised. Concerns expressed ... about how older people would cope with the responsibility of an Individual Budget were supported by the lower levels of well-being among older Individual Budget holders than the comparison group, as measured in the outcome interviews. This suggests that the anxiety and stress about potential changes to their established support arrangements reported by some older people in the qualitative interviews continued to moderate any potential gains from the increased transparency, control and flexibility offered by Individual Budgets. Evidence from the different strands of the evaluation suggests that older people often approach services at a time of crisis when they feel vulnerable or unwell and find decision-making difficult. The evaluation indicates that a potentially substantial proportion of older people may experience taking responsibility for their own support as a burden rather than as leading to improved control. Older people satisfied with their current care arrangements – particularly when this involved an established relationship with a current care worker – were reported to be reluctant to change, so differences in outcome would be minimal. Other attributes of older people, that have been shown to act as barriers to take-up of direct payments, are also likely to affect their responses to Individual Budgets. Older people's support plans reflected high levels of need for personal care rather than domains such as occupation and social participation, restricting the scope for improvements in wider well-being. The fact that older people received smaller average levels of Individual Budgets compared to younger adults was also likely to have limited their opportunities for flexibility and innovation.

The particular challenges of implementing Individual Budgets with older people make the care co-ordinator role notably demanding. At least in the early stages of the pilots, care co-ordinators were less experienced and less confident in developing more innovative and creative support plans with older people. Organisational arrangements to support the flexible deployment of care-managed 'virtual budgets' were generally not in place; changes to existing local authority contracts with providers that might facilitate greater flexibility for care managed 'virtual budget' holders had not been negotiated; and there was a lack of access to alternative deployment options and services that could bring greater flexibility and control without the well-documented drawbacks.

Glendinning et al. (2008: 238)

Other key findings included:

- the integration of different funding streams into an individual budget was the most difficult aim to achieve;
- transparency about resource allocation was essential, the researchers found that there was regional variation in how resources were allocated;

- Fair Access to Care Services was poorly aligned with funding streams;
- legitimate boundaries of adult care need to be reviewed because the focus and emphasis of personalisation are very different from care management – unless this is done it will stifle the scope for innovation and creativity.

Although the evaluation was hampered by a number of factors which included the relatively short follow-up period following implementation of individual budgets, the length of time which it took to set up an individual budget and that nearly a quarter of responses were from proxies, it nevertheless represents the first robust UK evaluation of this form of a personalised approach.

Critical thinking exercise 6.6

What do you think are the implications of the individual budget pilot conclusions for older people?

Does it mean that this social policy should be abandoned or reformulated so that it addresses the points the researchers raise?

Take a few moments to consider this. There is, of course, no definite answer to the question: it is a matter of opinion, but is certainly an issue worth considering if you are a practitioner in this field.

Abandonment of the current policy is very unlikely, in view of the variety of economic and political factors already outlined in this chapter and elsewhere in the book. Therefore the major policy question is what form services should take. What kinds of services are effective in meeting people's needs, bearing in mind all these wider considerations? In the next section we are going to look at what services may be feasible within current economic constraints.

Implementing personalisation: Applying policy to service development

The first point to make is that personalisation is still at an early stage and more work is needed at various levels. The kind of work that appears to be needed includes:

- making it much clearer to all involved who is eligible and who would benefit from personalisation;
- what is a legitimate use of public money in arranging care services;
- how resources are going to be shared so as to strike a balance between prevention and those in greatest need;
- making the mechanisms for accessing public support more transparent.

All of this needs to be led by central government, although implemented locally, since this is the standard model for delivery of community care services.

For older people in general, the picture as shown by this study is not particularly positive. One possible implication of this is that older people are at risk of faring less well as a result of personalisation than other groups of adult social care users. It would appear that older people are less likely to want the degree of responsibility which personalisation offers than other service user groups and that being given it may actually be harmful in some cases. This raises some interesting questions about the nature of empowerment and ageism which you are now invited to consider.

Critical thinking exercise 6.7

Consider the issue of empowerment and personalisation by thinking about the following questions.

- Is it best to consider all service user groups together or are the interests of older people better served by treating them as a discrete group?
- Is personalisation simply a mechanism for limiting state responsibility towards older people and a further extension of neo-liberalism?
- Alternatively, is personalisation a sound way of promoting people's rights and therefore respecting their rights as citizens, ensuring that they have basic needs met in line with social democratic thinking?
- What is a legitimate role for social work within this?

It would be well worthwhile debating these questions with fellow students. There are of course no definitive answers, but you should find the ensuing discussion quite stimulating. It is certainly topical and very real for all practitioners – not just in social work, but in health and social care more generally.

We are now going to look at some specific examples of the application of this policy to practice.

Partnership of Older People Project (POPP)

In addition to the individual budget pilots, the Partnership of Older People Project (POPP) is another main source of information as to how the themes associated with personalisation are working. The POPP initiative was set up to provide improved health and well-being for older people via a series of individual projects providing local services. These services were to be person-centred and integrated, to promote health, well-being and independence, and to prevent or delay the need for higher-intensity or institutional care.

POPPs ran in 29 local authorities from May 2006 to March 2009. In total, the 29 sites set up 146 core local projects, comprising many more individual services, aimed at improving health and well-being among older people and reducing social exclusion and isolation. The individual projects were determined according to local priorities. Of the 146 projects, two-thirds were primarily directed at reducing social isolation and exclusion or promoting healthy living among older people ('community facing'). The remaining one-third focused primarily on avoiding hospital admission or facilitating early discharge from acute or institutional care ('hospital facing'). Some addressed the full spectrum of needs. In addition to these 'core' projects, a further 530 small 'upstream' projects were commissioned from the third sector. Over a quarter of a million older people used the projects (Windle et al. 2010: vii).

Research summary

The evaluation of the projects reached the following conclusions.

- Health service efficiency gains were made particularly in relation to emergency care.
- POPP services generally had a beneficial impact on older people's lives.
- Social care managers were not happy with creating health savings from their budget. The difficulties associated with working across organisational boundaries also arose in the individual budget pilot studies.
- Primary care trusts have been the main source of sustainable financing.
- Poverty, illness and bereavement are the factors which have the most substantial impact on people's lives and within this context many projects, while beneficial, had limited impact.
- Involvement in the projects led to increased uptake in benefits.
- The older people who got involved with the projects as volunteers tended to be the newly retired, healthy and well educated.
- Small services providing practical and emotional help can have tangible benefits for older people's well-being.
- Systems need to be developed to support the decommissioning and recommissioning of services.

Windle et al. (2010)

It can be seen from the above that similar themes are apparent from the various projects involved in the early stages of personalisation. Looking at the details gives us some idea about what is meant by transformation. Essentially, in its most extreme form, it implies a dismantling of the institutional arrangements which have been developed over the last 60 years. Paradoxically the development of existing structures and institutions represents precisely the barriers to the full implementation of the vision of personalised care. At the heart of this may be some renegotiation of the relationship between the individual and the state – back to the debate between neo-liberalist and social democratic approaches to social policy.

Assistive technology

Telecare is specifically mentioned in *Putting People First* (HM Government 2007) as being integral to personalisation. Technology such as pendant alarms linked to call centres has been available for many years. The system works by the service user alerting a call centre that they require assistance so that the call centre can then get in touch with a nominated person to assist. This system has provided users and their families with greater peace of mind. Technology is developing all the time and now much more sophisticated monitoring systems are available, together with measures to reduce the risk associated with potentially dangerous appliances such as cookers. The technology now has the ability to monitor people's normal pattern of behaviour and to trigger an alert quite independent of the person doing anything themselves to call for assistance. The potential that this allows for people to remain in an independent environment is significant.

Below is an example of how Telecare can be applied in a situation in which the older person has dementia and suggests that the financial benefits can be significant when an individual is supported to maintain independence in their own home. The example comes from Northamptonshire.

Telecare supporting people with dementia

One project aims to support the independence of people with dementia by using technology to compensate for disabilities arising from dementia. Referrals to the project can be made by a social or health care professional, and a full assessment is undertaken, to identify technology tailored to meet specific needs. The project worker also has responsibility for obtaining and arranging for the installation of this technology, and liaising with the local control centre who co-ordinate any social response.

Risk management is a major feature of the project, for example, technology that can detect the presence of gas and isolate the supply to a cooker or fire that may have been left on unlit, and an alert can be raised. This means many people with dementia can continue to cook their own meals.

Key findings were that people without Telecare were four times more likely to leave the community for hospital or residential care over the 21 month evaluation period. The equivalent cost saving was £1.5 million over the 21 months.

Department of Health (2005a: 11)

Rural communities

Rural communities present particular issues when it comes to providing support for older people. Manthorpe and Stevens (2009), drawing on a range of studies, note that rural areas are experiencing the effects of an ageing society sooner than other parts of the country and as a consequence rural areas are likely to be those most substantially affected by changes to social care. The issues which the authors highlight, based on a small study conducted in 2008 regarding the impact of personalisation in rural communities, are as follows.

- The potential flexibility which personalisation offers might be appreciated by older people.
- There were concerns that local variations could affect the capacity to tailor support and to sustain developments.
- Long-term effects of personalisation need to be monitored and assessed to ensure equitable outcomes.
- The rural dimensions of adult social care need to be more rigorously explored.

Gloucestershire Village Agents Scheme is an example of one initiative designed to overcome some of the barriers faced by older people living in rural settings. The pilot phase of the scheme was held between 2006 and 2008. Village Agents support people over 50 years of age, bridging the gap between the local community and those statutory and voluntary organisations able to offer help or support where required. Working in 'clusters' of rural communities, Village Agents act as facilitators in the provision of high-quality information, promote access to a wide range of services, and identify unmet need within their community. Through training and access to appropriate information resources, the Village Agents develop their capacity to provide a service within their communities both in the short and longer term. A range of case studies illustrating the kind of intervention and support offered together with a full evaluation of similar initiatives can be found in Davis and Ritters (2009). These projects formed part of LinkAge Plus, which was sponsored by the Department of Works and Pensions and:

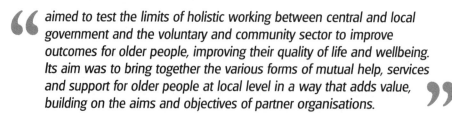

aimed to test the limits of holistic working between central and local government and the voluntary and community sector to improve outcomes for older people, improving their quality of life and wellbeing. Its aim was to bring together the various forms of mutual help, services and support for older people at local level in a way that adds value, building on the aims and objectives of partner organisations.

Davis and **Ritters** (2009: 1)

Implementing personalisation: Implications for social work practice

Critical thinking exercise 6.8

1. How will the social policy developments described in this chapter affect social work practice?

2. How is social work practice with older people in this 'transformed' service conceptualised by social policymakers?

3. How does this link to different social policy approaches, specifically the distinction between negative and positive freedom?

Write down some thoughts on each of these questions and then read on.

There can be no doubt that personalisation, a key component of the 'transformation' of adult care services, will have a major impact on social work practice with older people. For to put it bluntly, if older people or their representatives are going to undertake their own assessment and then arrange for the provision of their own services, what role is there for social work? In social policy terms, the policy appears to remove the need to have social workers working with older people at all. Some commentators have argued that, in light of the National Health Service and Community Care Act 1990, social work has become a victim of a growing separation between the aspirations for social work as a professional project and an administrative model (Ray et al. 2009). Arguably, it is precisely because social work practice has become a substantially administrative function that the question has now arisen about the necessity of having social workers at all. There is a curious paradox here: on the one hand the apparent aspirations of personalisation are to promote independence and choice, aspirations which are completely congruent with the professional value base, yet on the other hand the implication of the policy is to remove social work from the arena of supporting older people to achieve these goals.

So not unreasonably, you may have come to the conclusion that the thinking behind the policy of personalisation sees social workers as unnecessary to achieving the stated policy intentions. Furthermore, if we view social policy as a reflection of cultural norms, we see that the result may be empowerment interpreted as greater independence from social work intervention. Thus arguably, personalisation represents a step back by the state towards a more minimal role in the lives of older people. Returning to the ideas of positive and negative freedoms outlined in Chapter 2, we can thus see that personalisation represents an expansion of negative freedom, that is, it is consistent with greater freedom from state intervention in the detail of people's lives. But what of positive freedom?

Positive freedom, the ability to have certain basic needs met so that a person can engage in society, is an aspiration which lies at the heart of a number of definitions of what social work is concerned with. For example, the International Federation of Social Workers on their website state:

> *The social work profession promotes social change, problem solving in human relationships and the empowerment and liberation of people to enhance well-being. Utilising theories of human behaviour and social systems, social work intervenes at the points where people interact with their environments. Principles of human rights and social justice are fundamental to social work.*
>
> **IFSW** (2000 online)

This definition of social work is widely referred to in social work literature and also in a document published by the Department of Health entitled *The Future of Social Work in Adult Social Services in England* published in February 2010 (Department of Health 2010b). This paper was developed by all the key organisations involved in adult social care and emphasises the importance of social work thus:

> *Social work has a key role in the future of Adult Social Services. The purpose of adult social services and social work is to achieve better outcomes with adults of all ages who need services, support or protection. Social work is focussed on supporting independence, promoting choice and control for people facing difficulties due to disability, mental health problems, effects of age and other circumstances.*
>
> **Department of Health** (2010: 2)

In March 2010 the government published *Building a Safe and Confident Future*, a response to the Social Work Task Force review of social work. This reiterated that social work *helps adults and children to be safe, so that they can cope and take control of their lives again* in order to *make life better for people in crisis who are struggling to cope, feel alone and cannot sort out their problems unaided* (HM Government 2010: 5). This very simple definition is designed to aid public understanding of the social work role. It is also designed to reassert the value of social work, endorsing a raft of measures designed to raise the profile of social work and promote public confidence. Presumably this is intended to include work with older people.

It is difficult, at this stage, to come to some definitive conclusions about the social work role more generally in relation to older people. Some areas of activity are much more clearly articulated than others. Safeguarding and working with people in situations of complexity are highly probable areas of activity for social workers. This role sits comfortably within the realms of neo-liberalist, non-state intervention perspectives.

In this context social work concerns itself with those who have needs, which if not met, are likely to suffer gross deprivation or even death. What is less clear is the social work role in relation to co-production as a means of service development, capacity building, advocacy and prevention.

To return to Critical thinking exercise 6.8, you may have highlighted the kinds of activity noted at the end of the last paragraph. In order to empower older people, or to facilitate positive freedom, it is likely that the social work role will need to change from the bureaucratic care-management model which has dominated since the early 1990s. Too often care management has been care control. The strongest arguments put forward for this stem from the greater understanding of the economic and social costs of failing to intervene earlier, important in the context of impelling demographic factors and the current state of the global economy. These have been highlighted most recently in the Marmot Report *Fair Society, Healthy Lives* (Marmot 2010). If these arguments prevail, it does suggest that we may be entering into a new arena in which the sharp distinctions made between competing social policy perspectives may become blurred. Personalisation, for example, appears to try to steer a path between 'top-heavy' state intervention and the state vacating the field of care of older people altogether. In this sense it really is an example of a Third Way. An ongoing challenge will be how organisations and the individuals who work for them manage to co-operate. It is notable from both the individual budget and POPP (Partnership of Older People Project) evaluations that much development is still required for the concept of 'public good' to take precedence over managing a single organisation's budget and attaining specific targets.

In conclusion, we can say that personalisation certainly does not appear to be about providing an active deterrent to state support in the way that the workhouse was in the past (see case study in Chapter 2). Instead, it potentially allows for a discrete, individualised response to need, offering a wide range of services of different types and varying in quality. Yet nor does it have the same emphasis on market forces and bureaucracy in the way that care management, with its focus on large-scale commissioning, has had. However, on the downside, it does not provide for reliable forms of support outside of the family or market and is therefore not a collectivist approach. The emphasis is very much on the individual. Personalisation makes assumptions about people. The assumptions seem attractive, since they relate to the pursuit of individual aspirations, although with the coda that this also means being individually responsible. Scourfield (2007) develops this point, arguing that citizenship has been effectively defined as being active, responsible, entrepreneurial and enterprising and that these qualities are in turn linked to a concept of personhood. This raises questions about how the vulnerable, those who do not have these socially validated qualities, are going to be perceived.

The potential for increasing inequality is significant. It is not difficult to imagine that those people who have greater capacity in a general sense, for whatever reason, will be able to benefit more under personalisation than those who have less capacity. It is likely that social workers will be at this interface, working with the immediacy of people who are struggling to manage their independence and choice and whose dignity may be suffering. What remains to be seen is how far social workers will be able to engage with the longer-term capacity building and preventative aspirations of personalisation such as those highlighted by the Partnership of Older People Project.

Chapter Summary

The case study in this chapter was used to explore how the key 'transformation' policy, personalisation, might apply in practice. We started with an explanation as to why it was necessary to reconfigure (transform) services, connecting this to specific social policy developments exemplified in a number of government social policy documents: Department of Health (2005b, 2006, 2008, 2010b), HM Government (2007). We then unpacked the term 'transformation' by itemising its constituent parts in relation to community care: personalisation, self-directed support, individual budgets, resource allocation systems, and direct payments. This section concluded with a brief examination of research on direct payments, including some consideration of tentative reasons for its comparatively poor take-up by older people. The analysis then returned to the case study and applied personalisation to some specific scenarios. This enabled us to weigh up its benefits and limitations. This assessment continued in the next section, where personalisation was considered in relation to specific service developments. The general conclusion was that personalisation has considerable potential to promote empowerment, but this may not be as fully realised with older people as it might for other adult service-user groups. Finally the implications for social work practice were considered. This raised the tantalising question as to whether personalisation sounded the death knell for professional social work with older people or whether personalisation could only unleash its potential for offering real choices and a real say for older people if social work continued to play a major role, albeit in a different way.

The skills development elements of this chapter have centred on developing the ability to relate social policy developments to competing perspectives and then to conducting an evaluation of these. Throughout, the emphasis has been on encouraging you to formulate your own views on the basis of sound research evidence, which has also hopefully enabled you to understand how policy has a direct impact on social work practice with older people.

In the next, final, chapter you are going to be asked to think globally. We are going to consider approaches to social policy in a number of other countries and use these as the basis for conducting an assessment at the very broadest levels. Such an analysis helps to shed further light on social policy, social work practice and older people in the UK.

Further reading

Alcock, C., Daly, G. and **Griggs, E.** (2008) *Introducing Social Policy* (2nd edition). Harlow: Pearson Education Limited.
Useful basic social policy textbook which offers a broader introduction to the topics covered in this chapter.
Department of Health (2006) *Our Health, Our Care, Our Say: A New Direction for Community Services*. London: Department of Health.
Government policy paper on organisation of health and social care services.
Department of Health (2008) *Carers at the Heart of 21st-century Families and Communities*. London: Department of Health.
Government policy paper on support for carers.
Department of Health (2010b) *The Future of Social Work in Adult Social Services in England*. London: Department of Health.
Government policy paper specifically on role of social work in adult care services.
Glasby, J., Adult Health and Social Care in Bochel, H., Bochel, C., Page, R. and Sykes, R. (2009) *Social Policy: Themes Issues and Debates* 2nd edition. Harlow: Pearson.
One very relevant chapter in this commendable basic social policy text.
HM Government (2007) *Putting People First: A Shared Vision and Commitment to the Transformation of Adult Social Care*. London: Department of Health.
The key government policy statement on personalisation.
Lymbery, M. (2010) A new vision for adult social care? Continuities and change in The care of older people, *Critical Social Policy*. Vol. 30, No. 1, 5–26.
Article summarising and evaluating recent changes.
Marmot, M. (2010) *Fair Society, Healthy Lives: The Marmot Review*. London: Department of Health.
Useful summary of whole range of health-related equality issues.
SCIE (2010) *Personalisation: A Rough Guide* (revised edition). London: Social Care Institute for Excellence.
Excellent guide to personalisation, written primarily to assist practitioners.

7 Local and Global

Robert Johns

Introduction

In this chapter we are going to take a quick snapshot of some of the issues concerning
social work and social policy as they affect older people in other countries. Clearly in the
space available we are not going to be able to conduct some kind of comprehensive,
exhaustive international survey, but it will be interesting to see if some of the issues that
are of concern in the UK have parallels in other countries, and by implication whether
there are some lessons that UK social policymakers could learn.

The analysis begins by introducing you to some ways of comparing social policies in different countries. This part of the chapter is then divided into four subsections that incorporate consideration of some key questions.

1. The worldwide demographic social policy background: the global increases in population, and general ageing of the population. Are the challenges that confront UK social policymakers unique or is the 'ageing population' a global syndrome?
2. Comparison regarding the context in which social policy tries to address the needs of older people. Are the recent trends in UK social policy mirrored in the experiences of other countries? This is particularly pertinent in relation to financial provision for old age, given both the demographic and economic context. The imperative of making adequate provision for pensions is a major social policy concern. It raises questions about strategies that could be adopted to meet the financial needs of older people.
3. Consideration of the position of older people as providers and recipients of personal care as members of their own family. In some of the literature family care is specifically referred to as the issue of carers, but in many contexts and cultures this term is not recognised, so here we will talk primarily about family care, meaning non-state care. What do we learn from a comparison of the experiences of families caring for older people, and about the balance between family care and state care?
4. Health and well-being. What are some of the health-related issues for older people who live in other countries, or of older people from abroad who live in the UK?

As in previous chapters, we are going to explore some of these questions by means of a case study approach, but unlike previous chapters here the case studies are four fictional countries instead of individual families.

CASE STUDY 1

Ruritania is, as the name suggests, a rural country in which a significant proportion of the population are subsistence farmers, living off the land. Its taxes are comparatively low, and there are few services offered to older people by the state. The expectation is that families will care for their older relatives, who tend in the main to remain living with their adult children. If families are unable to cope, there are a few residential care homes run by charities or voluntary organisations, but there is no state funding to subsidise those places. In practice, few older people move into care as families regard caring for elders as an important family duty. People who live into their 80s and 90s are held in very high regard, respected as sources of wisdom.

CASE STUDY 2

Constantina is a country steeped in tradition, that prides itself on the quality of the health care it offers to all its citizens. It is a wealthy country, rich in natural resources, but with significant inequalities of wealth: those in employment are well-off, but those without jobs cannot rely on any kind of state support. All health and social care has to be paid for, but poorer families can approach various charities for assistance; these charities are well supported as donating to charity is seen as a religious and civic duty. The quality of services is variable but some are exceptionally good. They are run by the charities themselves although some are run by voluntary organisations on behalf of the state.

CASE STUDY 3

Urbanina is a city state, with many people employed in manufacturing industry and generally comprising small families or people living on their own. It has a number of residential homes for older people, many run by the municipal authorities but some offered by the private sector. Accommodation in the majority of them is in large dormitory-style accommodation with up to a dozen people sharing. Few personal possessions are allowed. Family members have to contribute to the fees their relatives have to pay in these homes. Provision of community services is patchy, with an expectation that families will care for older relatives until they decide that they can no longer do so.

CASE STUDY 4

Welfarania is a large country with a mixture of urban and rural populations. It is also rich in natural resources and for many years offered its citizens a wide range of employment opportunities in both the private and public sectors. It describes itself with pride as a welfare state. It offers a wide range of community care services to older people, including residential care as a very last resort. All services are funded by the state and all are of a high quality, with public guardians appointed to oversee older people's rights. Services are free, but have to be accessed through social workers on the basis of need; families are expected to care for older relatives if they can, but many elders now live some distance from their adult children.

These examples are, of course, fictional but they will be used to indicate how one might set about conducting some kind of comparative analysis.

Critical thinking exercise 7.1

Can you think of any countries that are similar to the countries being described?

Write down some ideas and then move on to the next section on comparing welfare regimes

---

Comparative analysis: Comparing welfare regimes

There a number of different approaches to conducting analytical social policy comparisons but by far the most significant was put forward by Esping-Andersen (1990, 1996). This classificatory approach has been termed 'regime theory' (Hill 2003: 254). Esping-Andersen puts forward three broad categories of welfare regimes which can be labelled as follows.

1. Liberalist, based on the kind of liberalist social policy approaches described in Chapter 2 and which returned in the 1980s as neo-liberalism (as described in Chapter 4). This promotes the notion of the free market economy, is strongly rooted in the principle of capitalistic free enterprise, and confines the state to the role of providing residual welfare – care for the most vulnerable only in extreme need, with use of welfare services being stigmatised.

2. Conservative or corporatist regimes are characterised by a belief in 'traditional values' such as conventional family arrangements, deference to political leaders (including royalty, if any) and strong respect for tradition. They differ from liberalist regimes in that the state may play quite an active role in people's lives but it is a benevolent role; for example, a royal family that pays for the establishment and running of a hospital to which the economically disadvantaged can have access.

3. Social democratic regimes, by contrast, promote equality in all its forms, often by means of an active redistribution of wealth through the taxation system or through provision of state welfare (services paid for by the rich but used predominantly by the poor). Such a regime would unashamedly call itself a welfare state and generally makes people's health and social care needs a top priority. There is a profound commitment to citizenship principles (see Chapter 3) and a positive view of freedom and the role of the state.

In order to clarify these differences you may find Table 7.1 useful. Please remember these relate to broad classifications, not to political parties.

Table 7.1: Analysing different approaches to social welfare and social work

	Liberalist	Conservative	Social democratic
Individualist or collective?	Individualism	Individuals with allegiances to others	Collectivism, pluralism
View of society	Society does not really exist, simply collection of individuals	Society is the country or culture to which one belongs, tradition-based, patriotic	Society important, has right to make provisions and policies which may override individual
View of political rights	People as individuals and rights to individual freedom	People have duties to each other and to their leaders	People as members of groups and rights as citizens
View of freedom	Individuals are free	Individuals subject to authority, which 'knows best'	Individuals not totally free, need help to articulate own needs and promote them
People's interests	People's interests are what they say they are	People's interests are the country's interests	People may not know what real interests are
View of equality and inequality	Inequality natural, price of reducing it far too high – infringes freedom	Inequality part of natural order but leaders do have duty to reduce more extreme inequalities	Inequality should be reduced as far as possible, welfare state is one means of achieving this
View of welfare state	Welfare state is gross infringement of liberty and interference with the free market	Welfare state useful in demonstrating leaders' concern for citizens of the country	Welfare state viewed as positive, main vehicle for implementing social policy
Role of social workers	Social workers interfere with people's basic freedoms, but are acceptable if they work for private sector or voluntary organisations	Social workers demonstrate the 'compassionate society', can be employed by benevolent state	Social workers are key people in tackling inequality, majority employed by the state, few employed in private or voluntary sectors
Economic form of social services	Commodified, i.e. services are bought and sold on open market as 'commodities'	Mixed economy: services can be provided on market basis or else can be provided by benevolent state	Decommodified, i.e. all state provision, no private provision of welfare services — cannot compete in quality or else proscribed

Critical thinking exercise 7.2

Now that you have been introduced to the typology, can you say into which category the case studies above fit?

You will note that there are four case studies but only three categories, so you may struggle to fit two into the same category or you may decide that you need a fourth category. So let's see how well the typology works.

Ruritania is a very traditional society, with respect shown to older people and a strong belief in traditional families. One can fairly confidently label this as a conservative regime, but note that the state plays a very limited role in people's lives so in that sense it is also a liberalist regime. Examples might include several countries in Africa, South America or southern Europe (southern Europe refers principally to countries such as Spain, Italy, Greece and Malta where the church still plays a major role in influencing social policy).

Constantina is 'steeped in tradition' with residualist welfare, since there is what seems to be a major role for charity. This is a classic conservative regime, although it too promotes some liberalist values. However, you would have to ask what would happen if the traditional values were challenged, in which case you might find this kind of state very active indeed. So such a regime is not really fully committed to liberalist core beliefs in freedom from state intervention. A number of Middle Eastern countries fit this category, although so too do some southern European and South American countries.

Urbanina might have presented you with a challenge, since there appear to be elements of residualism (liberalism) together with an important key role for the state as provider of care, albeit a rather outmoded model of residential care. So here we have a hybrid, which can often be the case with typologies. In fact the description is very loosely based on contemporary China, although it could also apply to Hong Kong and a number of other South East Asian countries. If you want to read more about this, there is a fascinating article by Chou (2010) which reports on the increasing difficulties experienced by Chinese families in providing care for elders, which has led to a growth in institutional care. However, this is not popular with older people, with only a small minority declaring themselves willing to live in such institutions.

Welfarania should have presented no difficulties whatsoever. Such a regime is clearly social democratic and several Scandinavian countries would correspond, more or less, to the description of this country (although note that even in countries such as Sweden there has been a move away from completely free state-run welfare services). There are, naturally, elements that would also apply to other countries, including the UK, but it would be rash to describe the UK as a truly social democratic country.

Critical thinking exercise 7.3

Which countries can you identify as fitting to each of the specific categories? What approach would they take to the care of older people? Where does the UK fit?

As we have just seen, the social democratic countries are quite easy to identify: any Scandinavian country will do. The state plays a major role in providing elder care, financing this out of general taxation.

Conservative-corporate states might include Belgium, Germany, France and Austria, all countries where entitlements to non-family support are based primarily on insurance systems. Sometimes insurance schemes are run indirectly by the state, i.e. contributions are compulsory but there is a choice of providers who are regulated by the state.

The classic example of a liberalist regime is the USA, where the state plays a minimal role in personal welfare generally and finances the care it does provide through taxation, but with provision strictly limited to those most in need, and always inferior in quality to what is provided in the private sector. The UK could also be classified in this way, although here the state plays a stronger role in providing for people's needs, so essentially the UK is a mixture.

So it may be best to think of the typology as indicating broad, general differences and ask the question: to what extent is this country liberalist, conservative or social democratic; what is the precise mix of these elements? An alternative approach, which may be even more effective, is to ask to what extent welfare services are commodified. As we saw in the chart above, in a free-market liberalist economy, all services are provided by private enterprise and are therefore commodities, whereas in a social democracy welfare state, services are completely 'decommodified'.

This enables us to locate the approach to social policy regarding older people and helps to understand the approach adopted in Britain, which assumes:

- the state has some role but broadly people are expected to contribute towards the costs of the services provided;
- families are regarded as having a duty to care for elders;
- access to services is determined on the basis of objectively assessed need, and is strictly rationed;
- a few services are decommodified, but for the majority of services for older people there has been a growing trend towards commodification, that is services being treated as commodities to be bought and sold on the open market.

Thus the UK is a hybrid, and as such is not that unusual. In an article that compared care of older people in the UK, the Netherlands and Taiwan, Chen reached the following conclusions.

All three countries seem to constitute hybrids of the Esping-Andersen welfare system typology. England can be identified as a 'liberal-social democratic' type of welfare regime which has limited elements of universal social democratic governance while the selective liberal element is rising. The Netherlands can be classified as a 'democratic-conservative' type of welfare, based on a general social security system with high social spending and is a more comprehensive welfare services model. Taiwan, like Japan, contains a 'liberal-conservative' welfare regime with the strong role of non-government organisations, as well as privileged occupational welfare.

Chen (2009: 2)

If we focus on expectations of the state, rather than simply the regime type, we may see the position more clearly. In a comparison of attitudes to state care in 11 European countries, Haberkern and Szydlik (2010) state the following.

In the so-called 'individualistic' countries of northern Europe, most people believe that the state should be the main provider of care. Normative obligations for mutual support between relatives are low, and parents do not want to become a burden on their children in their old age, or at least they do not expect them to provide substantial financial support or intensive personal care. In contrast, care is regarded as a family matter in Mediterranean and most central European countries.

Haberkern and **Szydlik** (2010: 303)

So in this sense there are similarities and differences with other countries. Let us now examine some other areas of similarities and differences.

Global demographic trends

Is the ageing population a global trend? Lawrence and Simpson (2009: 78) cite figures from various parts of the world to show that there are significant demographic discrepancies. While in much of northern Europe life expectancy continues to rise, in Russia life expectancy for men has fallen to age 59, while in sub-Saharan Africa many people live on average only into their early 40s. In western Europe the evidence points towards slow ageing of the population with static birth rates and slowly falling death rates, while in the USA, Canada and Australia this pattern is discernible but with significantly higher death rates in younger immigrant populations. China, meanwhile, is experiencing very rapid ageing of the population due to low birth rates combined with falling death rates (Holloway and Lymbery 2007: 376). Likewise Japan – although not quite to the same extent – has one of the highest life expectancy rates in the world at nearly 83 years (UN 2009: 6). The UN Report summarises the position as follows.

Globally the population of older persons is growing at a rate of 2.6 per cent per year, considerably faster than the population as a whole, which is increasing at 1.2 per cent annually. At least until 2050, the older population is expected to continue growing more rapidly than the population in other age groups ...

Marked differences exist between developed and developing regions in the number and proportion of older persons. In the more developed regions, over a fifth of the population is currently aged 60 years or over and by 2050, nearly a third of the population in developed countries is projected to be in that age group. In the less developed regions, older persons account today for just 8 per cent of the population but by 2050 they are expected to account for a fifth of the population, implying that, by mid-century, the developing world is likely to reach the same stage in the process of population ageing that the developed world is already at.

The pace of population ageing is faster in developing countries than in developed countries. Consequently ...

Today the median age for the world is 28 years, that is, half the world's population is below that age and the other half is above it. The country with the youngest population is Niger, with a median age of 15 years, and the country with the oldest is Japan, with a median age of 44 years. Over the next four decades, the world's median age will likely increase by ten years, to reach 38 years in 2050. At that time, the median age is expected to remain below 25 years in nine countries, most located in Africa, whereas the oldest populations are expected to be in Japan and Macao Special Administrative Region of China, whose median ages are projected to surpass 55 years.

The population of older persons is itself ageing. Among those aged 60 years or over, the fastest growing population is that of the oldest-old, that is, those aged 80 years or over. Their numbers are currently increasing at 4.0 per cent per year. Today, persons aged 80 years or over account for close to 1 in every 7 older persons (60 or over). By 2050, this ratio is expected to increase to nearly 1 person aged 80 or over among every 5 older persons.

UN (2009: x)

Critical thinking exercise 7.4

Reflect on the implications of all of this for social policy. Specifically, how would you complete the sentence in the quotation above that starts *Consequently ...* after *The pace of population ageing is faster in developing countries than in developed countries?*

Generally the consequences of this are mind-boggling. The major impact will concern financing pensions and services, since the proportion of working population to retirees will diminish. The figures are truly astonishing:

From 2009 to 2050, the ratio of persons aged 65 or over to those of working age is projected to grow from 6 per 100 to 11 per 100 in Africa, from 10 to 27 in Asia, from 10 to 31 in Latin America and the Caribbean, from 16 to 30 in Oceania, from 19 to 36 in Northern America and from 24 to 47 in Europe.

UN (2009: 20)

As a result, in relation to developing countries this creates a major challenge since they will have less time to adjust to the consequences and will have fewer resources with which to do so.

The global social policy context: The economics of ageing

Besides demographic factors, social policy needs to respond to rapidly changing economic conditions. The fast rise in wealth in the 1960s and early 1970s gave way to a major economic crisis that resulted in a significant economic recession in the 1980s. Likewise in 2007–8 another economic crisis occurred that will no doubt have long-lasting effects in terms of provision of publicly funded services. This global economic crisis inevitably created a number of social policy challenges and, with the additional factor of growth in numbers of older people, put a huge strain on the financial resourcing of pensions and services. This was common to many countries, and by way of exemplifying this, we are going to take two examples from different parts of the world.

First in South East Asia there are some resonances with the UK experience, but there are also some significant differences, as the following extract shows.

The preoccupation with economic development led to the welfare state being predominantly composed of social welfare programs for core industrial workers, while leaving the vulnerable sections of the population outside the system. Social policy tended to reinforce – rather than ameliorate – inequality in income and social strata. In terms of the political context, the developmental welfare state evolved in the context of authoritarian politics. Such attributes led to social grievances among low-income people, including farmers, informal sector workers, and other weak sections of the population. Nevertheless, the system was maintained, partly because of the authoritarian political regimes, and partly because of the sustained economic growth, which eventually trickled down to the lower strata of income groups. At the time of the economic crisis, it became clear that the developmental welfare state could not cope with social challenges in an economic downturn. In particular, the developmental welfare state was not able to tackle high unemployment since it assumed full employment.

Kwon et al. (2009: S15)

As a result, governments were obliged to respond, and did so in different ways. Hong Kong and Singapore maintained a selective approach, broadly speaking consistent with the liberalist social policy approaches, while Korea, Taiwan, Japan and Thailand began to move towards a more inclusive approach that would be more akin to a welfare state or social democratic approach (Kwon et al. 2009).

Critical thinking exercise 7.5

Read the extract above again and note any similarities and differences with the UK experience.

The first point relates to the emphasis on helping industrial workers at the expense of the more vulnerable. Although one could argue that the UK system does protect the most vulnerable, there is some evidence that echoes an emphasis on supporting people who work. One small example would be the increased pensions available to those who have contributed to earnings-related supplements, and also of course the fact that older workers are debarred from claiming employment-related benefits such as jobseekers' allowance.

The second point relates to social policy reinforcing rather than addressing inequalities. While one could write a whole book on this subject, one very relevant issue for older people is the extent to which the pensions system for the majority still leaves them in comparative poverty. That is, because state pensions are set at a flat rate they are pitched at a level that means that, unless a pensioner has other income from employer-provided retirement benefits, they may be obliged to claim some means of income support.

The third point that you may have identified relates to the economic downturn, and the fact that welfare state systems tend to rely on a continuation of full employment. This is currently a major policy issue. Unemployment is a 'double whammy' as far as the state is concerned since not only does a worker convert from a contributor to being a dependant overnight if they are obliged to claim benefits, but also they move from being someone who provides a significant amount of revenue to the government in the form of income tax, to someone whose tax burden is necessarily reduced because their income falls. Given that all the economics of provision of care for older people depend on a certain ratio of workers to dependent elders, even a slight shift in the balance can have a major impact. As we saw in the preceding section, this ratio is being changed anyway because of demographic factors, but economic changes will exacerbate this trend.

The second example comes from Sweden. Sweden has always been heralded as the exemplar of social democratic, welfare state countries. It has consistently pursued a social democratic approach to social policies since the 1930s and is noted for its strong commitment to inclusiveness, particularly gender equality, and a firm belief in the role of the state as a provider of universal benefits. Social policy in Sweden has a strong redistributive element. However, even Sweden, one of the wealthiest countries in the world, has not been immune from changes in the global economy.

Research summary

Summary of research concerning the financial experience of older Swedish people during the recession

Source: **Gustafsson** et al. (2009)

- The income of older Swedes has increased continuously since 1960.
- By 1990 the income standard of people aged 65–74 years was well over 90 per cent of those under 65 years of age.
- Real gross domestic product (GDP) fell by 5 per cent from 1990 to 1994.
- Taxes were increased and public transfer payments and outlays for public services were trimmed to limit the mounting deficits. Among the transfers that were trimmed were benefit payments to pensioners.
- New rights-to-work legislation has now raised the retirement age from 65 to 67.
- Around two-thirds of older people's aggregate income is from public pensions, which are therefore the main source of older people's total income.
- In recessionary times capital income became increasingly important as an income source for older people.
- Pension reform in 2003 reduced the previous high level of flat-rate benefit payable solely on the grounds of years of residence. Pensions are now taxable.
- Up to the 1990s pensions were index-linked to the rate of inflation; in the 1990s new systems were introduced to reformulate this indexation calculation and as a result there were effectively reductions in pensions.
- Despite this, *the real standard of living for older people in Sweden has increased steadily for several decades* (Gustafsson et al. 2009: 544).
- There have been dramatic changes in the distribution of real income since the end of the recession of the 1990s. The underlying trend is for increasing inequality among older people. In the decade following the end of the recession in the mid-1990s, inequality among older Swedes increased profoundly.
- Absolute poverty among older Swedes has declined significantly during the last quarter-century, yet when poverty is assessed in terms of a poverty line representing constant purchasing power, poverty among older people increased during the recession, reflecting benefit cuts and the cessation of full price indexation until 1999.
- The main cause of increased income inequality among older people was capital income. From 2001, *capital was the single strong driver of inequality* (Gustafsson et al. 2009: 556).

From this research it is possible to draw three principal conclusions.

1. The average income of older people was relatively stable during the deep recession of the first half of the 1990s. Consequently, their relative income position improved, but older people were by no means isolated from the downturn, as pensions were cut, full indexation was abandoned and taxes increased. In contrast, during the ensuing years of rapid economic growth, the income of older people did not increase as fast as the earnings of the economically active, and their relative position deteriorated.

2. With the reduction in benefits during the first half of the 1990s, a rising proportion of older people slipped under a poverty line based on fixed purchasing power. From 1998 until 2004, real income among the working-age population rose faster than the income of older people, leading to an increase in their relative poverty. Income inequality among older people in Sweden increased from the end of the recession in the 1990s.

3. Capital income is increasingly important for older people. It has led to an increasing inequality within this age group. One consequence of this is that older people are less homogenous as a group and this in turn has consequences for social services charges and for the mix between private and public provision and financing of services for older people. A substantial number of older people have difficulty making ends meet. They cannot afford to pay much for services and cannot access private healthcare or private social care.

Critical thinking exercise 7.6

Read the summary above again and consider what might be the parallels in the UK, and what lessons we might draw from this.

While you might well consider that Swedish provision is significantly more generous than that of the UK, some of the conclusions in relation to people's need to draw increasingly on capital reserves as income and their reduced capacity to pay for services are surely all telling factors.

As we saw from the discussion above, there is a reduction in the potential ability of the working-age population to pay for services due to both demographic and economic factors. At the same time there is a reduction in the potential ability of retired older people to pay for services, and this is a factor which appears to be significantly underplayed in current social policy debates. As taxpayers who are also potential beneficiaries of services, we need to consider how governments might respond to this.

Family care or state care?

We stay in Sweden for the next example of a comparative analysis, focusing this time on that all-important partnership between the state and the family in providing care for older people. The question asked by social policy analysts in Sweden was simply whether it was always a question of care for older people being either family-based or publicly provided (Sundström et al. 2006). In a detailed evidence-based analysis of the kinds of services Swedish older people use, the researchers reached the following conclusions.

It has been argued that family care – and maybe the family itself – is in decline in welfare-state countries, as exemplified in Sweden. Whilst this may be true of basic financial support and in providing housing, it seems not to be true of care in a narrower sense, giving help with everyday household tasks and personal care ... Surveys in Sweden and several other countries have demonstrated that family members have neither abdicated from their responsibilities nor wish to do so. There is increasing evidence that the desired situation is one of shared responsibility, and that these views are held by older people themselves, the general population and, most pertinently, among those with an elderly parent in need of help and who receives family care ...

It is difficult to interpret patterns of care, but it seems that improved housing, more assistive technologies and other resource increases (notably more education) since the late 1980s have eased the daily lives of older people, although their health has only marginally improved. Their ability to manage household tasks has improved remarkably, but the need for personal care has improved much less ... It is likely that Sweden has seen long-term 'reverse substitution', that is that some of the care that for decades was provided by the state has now been 'taken over' by the family.

Sundström et al. (2006: 777, 779)

This notion of 'reverse substitution' confirms some of the researchers' previous findings (Johansson et al. 2003):

Substitution among the providers of old-age care has usually meant a process whereby the state 'takes over' what families used to do, but during the 1980s and 1990s, both home help and institutional care were cut back substantially in Sweden as elsewhere ... It emerges that increased inputs from families match the decline of public services, that is, a 'reverse' substitution has recently been taking place.

Johansson et al. (2003: 269)

The key role that family care plays is underlined in a recent overview of family care across the whole of Europe (Glendinning et al. 2009). This found that across the European Union, family members provided by far the greatest amount of care for older people, and indeed states rely on family care in order to make the welfare of older people sustainable. The researchers' estimates were that across the European Union in 2005, 19 million people aged 25 and over provided at least 20 hours a week care for an older person or a disabled or chronically ill person. Around 9.6 million of them provided at least 35 hours a week care. There were very wide variations in informal care arrangements, attitudes towards the balance between the state and family provision, and availability of services. Carers in Mediterranean and Eastern European countries experienced a lower 'quality of life' compared with those in countries with developed welfare services such as the UK and Scandinavia. Yet there was one feature common to all countries: women formed the majority of those who were the providers of care and also, perhaps less predictably, the recipients of care.

This difference between southern Europe and northern Europe was confirmed in a survey of carers' attitudes across Europe. This found:

 Intergenerational care is more prevalent in southern and central European countries, where children are legally obligated to support parents in need, and care is perceived as a responsibility of the family, whereas in northern Europe, the wider availability of formal care services enable adult children, particularly daughters, to have more choice about their activities and use of time.

Haberkern and **Szydlik** (2010: 299)

Critical thinking exercise 7.7

Is there any evidence of 'reverse substitution' in the UK? Do you think it would be feasible to re-create expectations that adult children would provide care for their own ageing parents?

There are of course no easy answers to this, although it may pay you to revisit Chapter 4, which charted the move away from a state-dominated system of provision towards a mixed economy, which included a significant element of family care. So although on the surface it may seem unlikely that expectations of the state might be reversed, the evidence from Sweden suggests it can be, and clearly in southern Europe family obligations are reinforced and sometimes enshrined in statute.

Before moving on from family care, it is important to note one major difference between the European experience and experience in other parts of world. European-based research and analyses have focused predominantly on older people as recipients of care, whereas increasingly commentators on the experiences of older people in Africa focus on the unanticipated expectations of older people to become providers of care, compelled to assume full-time care of their grandchildren. The primary cause of this is HIV AIDS (Ice et al. 2010; Munthree 2010).

Health and well-being

Included in this section are social issues related to health and well-being such as social isolation, which naturally connects to mental health. We start with a worldwide overview of health issues relevant for older people.

A research summary by Holloway (2009) focuses on life-threatening health problems for older people and end-of-life care. It cites statistics from the World Health Organisation that indicate that the major threat to life for the majority of older people in the world is cardiovascular disease, particularly for women in the oldest age group. In poorer areas of the world, communicable diseases are the second and third most common causes of death, but cancer is also high up on the list of health issues for all people. For older people compared with the general population, Alzheimer's and Parkinson's diseases are much more prevalent, and falls are a significant problem for older people, especially women over 80. As people are living longer, so they need more support from health and social care services, although it has to be noted that in many of the poorer countries in the world, lack of basic healthcare resources continues to be a serious impediment.

Holloway points out that a major issue for older people is the degree to which their wishes are taken into account as they approach the end of their lives. In the Western world the overwhelming view among older people is that they want to die at home, yet in fact very few older people in Europe, the USA or Australia do actually die there, with those in the oldest age group, women and people who live alone being the least likely to have their wishes fulfilled. Conversely, older people are less likely than other age groups to have access to hospice care or palliative community care services. Right across the globe there is a picture of older people not being involved in advance care planning decisions, although consistently older people want to be with family and the people they love at the very end of their lives. The social policy implications for service providers are:

 to accommodate a culturally appropriate role for the family within formal service provision rather than to attempt to shore up the care provided by an overburdened carer who may also be old and frail.

Holloway (2009: 719)

Worldwide, a major preoccupation is the affordability of healthcare. In March 2010 the US House of Representatives voted for major healthcare reform of the predominantly private system that operates in the USA. Such a system relies on people taking out health insurance to fund all forms of healthcare including hospitals, although for over-65s this is supplemented by Medicare, which subsidises healthcare and is funded by the federal government. One driver for reform is the high comparative cost of healthcare in the US compared with other countries. The Organisation for Economic Co-operation and Development (OECD) offers the following information related to this.

Total health spending accounted for 16.0 per cent of GDP in the United States in 2007, by far the highest share in the OECD. Following the United States were France, Switzerland and Germany, which allocated respectively 11.0 per cent, 10.8 per cent and 10.4 per cent of their GDP to health. The OECD average was 8.9 per cent.

The United States also ranks far ahead of other OECD countries in health spending per capita, with spending of 7,290 USD in 2007, almost two-and-a-half times greater than the OECD average of 2,984 USD (adjusted for purchasing power parity). Norway follows with spending of 4,763 USD per capita, then Switzerland with spending of 4,417 USD per capita. Differences in health spending across countries reflect differences in price, volume and quality of medical goods and services consumed.

The public sector is the main source of health funding in all OECD countries, except Mexico and the United States. In the United States, 45 per cent of health spending was funded by public sources in 2007, a much lower share than the average of 73 per cent for OECD countries

OECD (2010 online)

Critical thinking exercise 7.8

What are the key differences between the US and the UK systems?

The US system contrasts markedly with that in the UK, where 82 per cent of health spending was funded by public sources, well above the average for all OECD countries of 73 per cent (OECD 2010 online). Consequently in the UK people expect to be able to access all forms of healthcare without concern about the cost; only a small minority of the population take out private healthcare or access private health services. All healthcare is free at the point of delivery, although people do expect to pay for prescriptions and optical and dental care.

Hence the UK can be seen as the complete opposite of the US system, but as an example of a system that tries to amalgamate both public and private spending there is the example of Singapore, a dual system. Here healthcare is financed by a combination of taxes, employer medical benefits for employees, private insurance, compulsory savings and direct payments by patients. Public health services cater for lower-income groups. The principles underpinning the health system have been operating for many years and are held to be important in that country, being dedicated towards the promotion of good health and 'responsible' attitudes. There is both public provision and market competition, with the inevitable results in inequalities and comparatively high percentage of household expenditure on medical care. Subsidies for health are provided by Medisave, Medishield and Medifund, which are combinations of compulsory saving schemes and state-run charity but all face challenges of health costs exceeding the ability to pay (Reisman 2009). This naturally raises fundamental questions about affordability and long-term sustainability of the present system, a theme which is effectively global.

In other parts of the world, inequality of access to healthcare is also an issue. For example, in one study of six Caribbean countries there were wide disparities found in responses to the ageing population, together with unequal access to healthcare, social services, public transport, income and food, depending not surprisingly on the socioeconomic status of the older person (Cloos et al. 2010). Furthermore, home care services were either insufficient or nonexistent. Welfare benefits did not provide adequate income and some older people simply did not have enough income to be able to afford to eat. While some people received support from relatives, others were affected by isolation and deprivation.

Social isolation and depression also featured in the lives of many older people in the Midwest of the USA surveyed by Jeon and Dunkle (2009). This was a longitudinal study examining depression among the 'oldest old' age group. The researchers tentatively suggested that depression might be linked to ongoing concerns about health and health-related issues which had a cumulative effect on mental health. One factor that appears to forestall the depression was the degree of mastery which a person had over events in their lives, which is taken to mean the degree of control they had over everyday decisions and contacts. Meanwhile research in Canada suggested that what contributed to older people's sense of well-being was the extent to which they engaged in voluntary activities (altruistic behaviour) and what is called 'social capital'. Social capital is taken in this context to mean a sense of belonging to a community, degree of neighbourhood trust, and potential for participation in group activities. There was a statistically significant correlation between altruistic behaviour and well-being.

> Specifically, our key findings suggest that those with a strong sense of community are not only likely to be happier but also to experience increased life satisfaction ... governments need to provide concrete structural supports for older volunteers with opportunities for learning rather than viewing them as unpaid workers. Providing them with social roles allows them to be active contributing members of society. From a health promotion perspective, establishing volunteerism in older adults as a public health issue may be a vital step towards promoting healthy ageing.
>
> **Theurer** and **Wister** (2010: 177–8)

To complete this section, let's return to the UK and consider the experience of older people who have migrated from other countries. You will find a number of case examples discussed in Chapter 6 of *Introducing International Social Work* (Lawrence et al. 2009). There was also a section on black and minority ethnic elders in Chapter 5 of this book. So here we are just going to explore one example: older Chinese people living in the UK. One reason for this selection is that Chinese people experience different cultural approaches to health and social care. For example, in a review of the sensitivity of UK health services to Chinese origin older people, Chau and Yu (2010) start by discussing how Chinese older people generally view health and health improvement and their strategy for adapting to incorporating different ways of organising health within a foreign culture. It concludes that making services sensitive to the diverse needs of the minority groups involves more than just documenting their healthcare needs. Healthcare services need to be made 'user centred and needs oriented' (Chau and Yu 2010: 398).

In a survey of Chinese people's attitudes towards the welfare state, one survey based on quantitative data revealed that 81 per cent of respondents believed that adult children should take care of their parents, with 59 per cent believing that they should also meet older people's financial needs (Chau et al, 2007). Not surprisingly, the dominant characteristic that came out of this survey was a strong belief in self-reliance within a family-orientated context, with low expectations of public welfare and some disagreement that taxes should be raised in order to pay for the welfare state. In this context it is understandable that Chinese older people are underrepresented as recipients of welfare state services, but there is also the danger that services may not be provided when they are desperately needed because of assumptions about Chinese families' self-reliance.

An investigation that focused on Chinese women (Cook 2010) confirmed this, although there were interesting differences between generation groups. This is partly because of migration patterns: the oldest group of people surveyed had often already retired when they came to the UK to join their children. In the main they had migrated from rural areas of China and spoke little English. They had few expectations of health and social care, and were surprised and pleased with the quality of services they received. By contrast, younger Chinese women were prepared to be more critical of services. The older group also experienced a dramatic drop in status, since moving to the UK meant they were dependent on family to interpret for them, to guide them through systems, and generally they considered themselves to be a burden on their families (Cook 2010: 266).

Social policy therefore needs to take into account the different life experiences of older people, and the importance of differentiating distinct groups even within minority ethnic groups cannot be overstated. Such differentiation may reveal inequalities and disparities in health and income, a key factor that it is all too easy to overlook (Moriarty and Butt 2004).

Chapter Summary

The case studies in this chapter were imaginary countries rather than people, and were used to demonstrate one method of comparing countries' social policy regimes — the Esping-Anderson characterisation of regimes as liberalist, conservative/corporatist or social democratic. We concluded that no country fits exactly into one of the three divisions in the typology, but that the typology had value in demonstrating fundamental differences of approach. In many cases, countries were hybrids, and this is particularly true in the case of the United Kingdom.

We then explored a comparative analysis of different countries using four headings: global demographic trends, the economic position of older people, family care versus state care, health and well-being.

Under the first heading we considered the extent to which the demography of an ageing population was common to all countries of the world, and concluded that it was but in different ways. There are internationally huge disparities in life expectation, but in all countries the proportion of older people compared with the working population is increasing, and this changing ratio will place significant demands on all countries in terms of financing services for older people. This includes especially developing countries for which this will become an acute problem very quickly in a few years' time.

We then considered the economic position of older people with particular reference to the effects of economic recessions. Building on the experiences of the recession of the early 1990s, we explored the various ways in which older people were affected, and this may help us to predict how they will fare under a more austere economic climate which may well include a contraction of services. There are of course parallels between this and the demographic issue, and it is clear that the growth in ageing population together with recessionary economic forces may make life really tough for some older people. There are obvious social policy challenges in all of this.

Under the third heading we considered the issue that is common to all countries, namely what is the balance between the role of the state and the role of the family in providing care for elders. Again there are huge disparities here, some of them linked to cultural differences, but we also had an example of a reversal of policy in Sweden, where there is some evidence to suggest that there was 'reverse substitution', that is, the family being drawn back into providing care that the state had provided hitherto.

Under the final heading of health and well-being, we drew on some international data on the health of older people and discovered a number of common strands. There was also some consideration of different approaches to healthcare, with a very stark contrast between the USA and the UK in this respect. Finally under this heading we considered briefly the experience of older people in the UK who have migrated from other countries. Given that this is well covered elsewhere, we focused our attention solely on the experience of older Chinese people, since this revealed significant cultural differences, which led us to conclude that social policy needs to take into account not only the diversity of older people, but also of significant differences within minority ethnic groups.

The skills development elements of this chapter have focused on evaluating different perspectives and ideas, of which there were quite a number in this chapter, including applying a typology, and reflecting on similarities and differences between the British welfare system and that of other countries. You were also invited to consider the implications of global trends for UK social policy, and from all of this it will become clear that there are some urgent questions that need to be addressed by policymakers which will inevitably have significant consequences for social work.

Further reading

Cook, J. (2010) Exploring Older Women's Citizenship: Understanding the Impact of Migration in Later Life. *Ageing and Society*, 30: 253–73.
An article that compares experiences of the welfare state in the UK, focusing on women who have migrated from different countries.

Esping-Anderson, G. (1996) *Welfare States in Transition.* London: Sage.
A wide-ranging comparative analysis that compares the responses of different countries across the globe to the 'welfare state crisis'.

Hill, M. and Irving, Z. (2009) *Understanding Social Policy* (8th edition). Oxford: Wiley-Blackwell.
Chapter 11 focuses on the UK in the wider world, exploring global issues. Chapter 11 of the seventh (2003) edition also has the same focus.

Lawrence, S. et al. (2009) *Introducing International Social Work.* Exeter: Learning Matters.
Includes a chapter on older people but also worthwhile as an introduction to a global approach to social work more generally.

Moriarty, J. and Butt, J. (2004) Inequalities in Quality of Life Among Older People from Different Ethnic Groups. *Ageing and Society*, 24: 729–53.
A widely quoted article that is probably more relevant for social work than social policy students. It analyses inequalities within different ethnic groups, arguing that more attention ought to be paid to these inequalities rather than just different ethnicities.

UN (2009) *World Population Ageing.* New York: United Nations Department of Economic and Social Affairs Population Division.
Fascinating statistical data enabling comparisons between all countries to be made. Downloadable from UN Website at www.un.org

competitive tendering, and commissioning services. Politically, belief in egalitarianism was challenged by Hayek and others who believed that equality was incompatible with personal freedom, accepting social inequality as natural, rather like the weather, pointing out that the market is neutral, although the consequences of market forces may be that some prosper while others do not.

After our developmental and historical overview, incorporating the key ideas that undergirded the changes, in Chapter 5 we looked at the social policy challenges of providing for the whole variety of groups of older people to be found in contemporary society. Compared with earlier periods, by far and away the most significant challenge to the case study derives from two demographic trends: the general increase in the older population (particularly the 'oldest old') and the diversity in that population that arises principally as a consequence of migration. As far as our case study is concerned, therefore, we can now say that in contrast to a century ago, the situation described would be fairly common. We can also say that there is important information missing from the case study which we would now need: we are not told about ethnicity, or provided with any information about the social background of Stella and Beatrice. In order to provide appropriate services, we would need that information since it is now considered that social policy should be directed to the end of meeting the needs of a hugely diverse population.

Chapter 6 introduced the topical feature of current social policy, personalisation. What would this mean for the two people in our case study? Primarily it would suggest that services should be fitted around the person, which implies that a broad range of services needs to be potentially available from which a choice can be made. Who should make that choice? This is where policy is shifting towards indicating that it is the service users themselves who should be exercising choice, but with advice and guidance if they need it. The only really effective way of exercising choice is to have the financial wherewithal to do so, hence the policy drive towards increased use of individual budgets and direct payments. In the chapter we were introduced to the debate about these, and some reservations about whether it was right to push people into management responsibility for commissioning services they need. Much of this chapter was given over to an examination of research evidence concerning implementation of personalisation, but it is important also to remember the wider context and the scepticism in some quarters that suggests that personalisation is a policy popular with policymakers who want to avoid criticism of services and budgeting priorities, since they can now argue that the service user makes the choice of services and priorities themselves.

Chapter 7 broadened the discussion from the local, the UK context, to the global. In order to compare social policy in different countries, we considered the use of a typology that classifies welfare 'regimes', drawing out broad distinctions labelled as liberalist, conservative, and social democratic. This facilitated an analysis of social policy in Britain, which in effect is a mixture of all three elements, and differs significantly from some countries such as the USA, which is almost exclusively liberalist, and the Scandinavian countries, which are firmly wedded to social democratic principles. In our global considerations we next considered the extent to which the demographic trends in Britain had been replicated throughout the rest of the world. The conclusion was that they certainly did correspond to the trends in other countries of Europe, North America and parts of East Asia. Here there is a preoccupation with the demographic imbalance created by the 'ageing' population. This stands in marked contrast to other countries, particularly in Africa, where there is a much higher proportion of young people; this poses different challenges also linked to an imbalance, in this case created by the comparatively high birth rate and much higher mortality rates for older adults. For Britain, as elsewhere, one genuine policy concern therefore is affordability: with an expanding older age group and a contracting working group, how is the necessary revenue to pay for health and social care services to be raised?

This raises the issue from the case study of the role of the state and the role of the family in providing care for older people, a theme that has been running right through this book. From the non-intervention of the Edwardian era, we have travelled through the introduction of the state-dominated welfare state, followed by the mixed economy, and we have now reached a time when, due to unremitting external factors, major fundamental questions need to be urgently addressed concerning family responsibility, the role of the state and the role of social work in promoting the welfare of older people.

Answers to selected Critical thinking exercises

Critical thinking exercise 2.3

Key ideas	Influences on current policy: Social work practice and older people examples
Freedom (freedom from state interference, individual freedom)	Right to live independently, to make own provisions for old age, no compulsion to accept care or services, right to be eccentric and choose one's own lifestyle, right to choose service providers
Free market forces (prices regulate markets, the law of supply and demand)	Competition between service providers, consumer choice, pensions linked to investment performance, ability to purchase care, inequalities of wealth
Individualism (individual responsibility and accountability)	Assumption that people will make arrangements for old age, responsibility of immediate family to care, services geared to supplementing support from family and carers
Role of government (residual but strong on defence and law and order)	Basic state pension comparatively low level, means tested benefits, assessment of needs, constraints on state financed support services

Critical thinking exercise 3.8

Key ideas	Influences on current policy: Social work practice and older people examples
Positive freedom: freedom to participate fully in society	Right to have basic needs met, to expect state to make provisions for old age, to expect care services to be provided to maintain independence
Mixed economy: state sector, private and independent sector	State is main provider of services, can result in limited choice as voluntary and private sectors unable to compete, pensions provided in accordance with government regulations determined by Parliament, state pays for care, reduced inequalities of wealth
Collectivism: people are responsible for each other	Assumption that government will make arrangements for old age on people's behalf, responsibility of state to provide care where family cannot or will not, services readily available alternatives to family and carers
Role of government as major provider of welfare	Basic state pension intended to be at level at which older people can live comfortably, benefits as of right rather than means tested, based on insurance principle, establishing need triggers automatic provisions regardless of income, acceptance of state financed support services paid for through National Insurance or taxation

Putting the Chapter 2 and Chapter 3 Critical thinking exercises together

Influences on current policy: Liberalism	Influences on current policy: Social democracy (citizenship) and Keynesianism
Right to live independently, to make own provisions for old age, no compulsion to accept care or services, right to be eccentric and choose one's own lifestyle, right to choose service providers	Right to have basic needs met, to expect state to make provisions for old age, to expect care services to be provided to maintain independence
Competition between service providers, consumer choice, pensions linked to investment performance, ability to purchase care, inequalities of wealth	State is main provider of services, can result in limited choice as voluntary and private sectors unable to compete, pensions provided in accordance with government regulations determined by Parliament, state pays for care, reduced inequalities of wealth

Assumption that people will make arrangements for old age, responsibility of immediate family to care, services geared to supplementing support from family and carers	Assumption that government will make arrangements for old age on people's behalf, responsibility of state to provide care where family cannot or will not, services readily available alternatives to family and carers
Basic state pension comparatively low level, means-tested benefits, assessment of needs, constraints on state-financed support services	Basic state pension intended to be at level at which older people can live comfortably, benefits as of right rather than means-tested, based on insurance principle, establishing need triggers automatic provisions regardless of income, acceptance of state-financed support services paid for through National Insurance or taxation

Critical thinking exercise 4.3

Keynesian	Monetarist
Government should concentrate on the demand side	Government should concentrate on the supply side
Government should invest in public spending to increase employment	Government should cut public spending in order to reduce the money supply
Government should control the amount of currency in circulation or control the rate at which banks lend	No need to interfere with currency, market forces should prevail, and these will determine bank lending rates
Poverty can be addressed since increasing poorer people's demand for goods and services creates employment	Creating artificial demand for goods and services simply causes inflation, which has harmful effects on people in poverty
Redistribution of wealth is desirable if it enables more people to purchase goods and services	Redistribution of wealth represents an acceptable interference with market forces
Redistribution can take the form of provision of public services	Public expenditure should be cut drastically in order to reduce the money supply
Overall, the economy should be a balanced 'mixed economy'	Public sector should be open to market forces: internal market should be created, private sector should provide wherever possible

Critical thinking exercise 5.8

	Liberalist	Social democratic
Diversity	Differences seen as natural. No need perceived for state intervention. Independent sector services will emerge that meet the needs of diverse communities and therefore reflect the different needs.	State has a duty to ensure that services respond to diversity of need. Differences sometimes seen as problematic. State must ensure all have equal access to services that are responsive to cultural differences.
Age discrimination	People should be free to choose when to retire. Employers may or may not engage older workers, it is up to them although it will often be in their interest to do so as older workers are more reliable and may be cheaper.	State should legislate to prohibit age discrimination. Alternatively there may be a national retirement age imposed on everyone (effectively equality of discrimination).
Social exclusion	Encourage families to care for each other, encourage self help and community enterprise.	Develop range of government policies to address all aspects of social exclusion.
Poverty	Making arrangements for old age is individual's responsibility. Lack of savings and foresight may result in relative poverty.	State has a duty to provide sufficient income to ensure older people are not poor.
Health and disability	Emphasise individual responsibility to safeguard against ill-health through insurance. Promote family care and philanthropy.	Provide state-run health service with uniform standards to ensure that all have equal access to healthcare.
Older carers	Applaud their efforts since they provide ideal role model of expectations of responsible members of society. If in receipt of services, encourage to manage these themselves, for example, through direct payments.	Provide support services funded by the state. If necessary take over their role and provide direct care. Ensure uniformity of standards of assessment and service provision. State makes decisions about services provided in each individual case.

Appendix:
Critical Thinking Exercises and Key Ideas

Now that you have reached the end of the book, you may want to review not just the content, but the skills you have acquired. So what follows is a list of all the Critical thinking exercises undertaken in each of the chapters, a summary of what you were asked to do, and a correlation with the core skills, to which you were introduced in the opening chapter. These were:

- skill 1   demonstrating understanding and application of theoretical ideas
- skill 2   comparing and contrasting different viewpoints and experiences
- skill 3   relating different views to underlying philosophies or ideologies
- skill 4   evaluating different perspectives and ideas
- skill 5   evaluating evidence
- skill 6   synthesising arguments
- skill 7   reflection
- skill 8   reviewing, re-evaluating and reformulating your own views

Critical thinking exercise 1.1	skill 1	Identifying significant factors in case study	☐
Critical thinking exercises 1.2, 1.3	skill 1	Summarising research and social policy analyses, considering implications for social work	☐
Critical thinking exercise 1.4	skill 1	Connecting social policy to ideology	☐
Critical thinking exercise 1.5	skill 4	Grouping different ideas together	☐
Critical thinking exercise 1.6	skill 4	Connecting social policy to the role of the social worker	☐
Critical thinking exercise 2.1	skill 2	Compare the experience of older people in Edwardian times with today	☐
Critical thinking exercise 2.2	skill 1, skill 4	Using explanatory theories	☐
Critical thinking exercise 2.3	skill 3	Connecting key ideas to social work practice	☐
Critical thinking exercise 3.1	skill 2	Comparing experiences	☐

Critical thinking exercise 3.2	skill 3	Drawing up glossary	☐
Critical thinking exercise 3.3	skill 4	Connecting social policy to theory	☐
Critical thinking exercise 3.4	skill 2, skill 4	Researching connections and comparing experiences	☐
Critical thinking exercise 3.5	skill 1	Constructing a systematic analysis	☐
Critical thinking exercise 3.6	skill 3	Connecting ideas and theories to practice	☐
Critical thinking exercise 3.7	skill 1	Connecting theories to people's lived experiences	☐
Critical thinking exercise 3.8	skill 2, skill 4	Comparing and contrasting theories	☐
Critical thinking exercise 4.1	skill 2	Comparing experiences	☐
Critical thinking exercise 4.2	skill 1	Evaluating competing theories	☐
Critical thinking exercise 4.3	skill 4, skill 6	Comparing theories	☐
Critical thinking exercises 4.4, 4.5	skill 3	Connecting theories to social policy	☐
Critical thinking exercises 4.6, 4.7	skill 3	Connecting practice principles to competing theories and explanations	☐
Critical thinking exercise 5.1	skill 2	Relating social policy to case study	☐
Critical thinking exercises 5.2, 5.3	skill 8	Identifying implications of social policy	☐
Critical thinking exercise 5.4	skill 5	Analysing data	☐
Critical thinking exercise 5.5	skill 7	Analysing social policy and discrimination	☐
Critical thinking exercises 5.6, 5.7	skill 7	Reflecting on social exclusion and older people	☐
Critical thinking exercise 5.8	skill 3	Compare and contrast theories and their application	☐
Critical thinking exercise 6.1	skill 3	Explaining change in social policy	☐

Critical thinking exercise 6.2	skill 7	Reflection on language and social policy	☐
Critical thinking exercise 6.3	skill 5	Evaluating evidence	☐
Critical thinking exercises 6.4, 6.5, 6.6	skill 8	Assessing merits and shortcomings of policy	☐
Critical thinking exercise 6.7	skill 8	Considering policy alternatives	☐
Critical thinking exercise 6.8	skill 7	Connecting social policy to practice	☐
Critical thinking exercises 7.1, 7.2, 7.3	skill 4	Comparing and contrasting perspectives and policies	☐
Critical thinking exercises 7.4, 7.5	skill 5	Evaluating evidence	☐
Critical thinking exercise 7.6	skill 8	Exploring social policy implications	☐
Critical thinking exercise 7.7	skill 7, skill 8	Analysing relationship between state and individual	☐
Critical thinking exercise 7.8	skill 2	Comparing and contrasting approaches to social policy	☐

In this book you have also been introduced to some Key ideas that underpinned social policy developments. These were:

Key idea 2.1	Liberalism	Explained in Chapter 2.	☐
Key idea 2.2	Social Darwinism	Explained in Chapter 2.	☐
Key idea 2.3	Scientific rationalism	Explained in Chapter 2.	☐
Key idea 3.1	Collective responsibility and state intervention in welfare	Explained in Chapter 3. Further discussion on state intervention in Chapters 6 and 7.	☐
Key idea 3.2	Keynesian economics: state intervention in the economy	Explained in Chapter 3. Also discussed in Chapter 7 in relation to other countries.	☐

Two further major ideas have been highlighted.

Citizenship	Explained in Chapter 3.	Also discussed in Chapter 7 in relation to other countries.	☐
Social democratic ideas	Explained in Chapter 3.	Also discussed in Chapter 7 in relation to other countries.	☐

Glossary

Ageism	Discrimination on basis of age, usually including negative assumptions made about people on age grounds (any age, not just older people)	Explained in Chapter 1, and key area of discussion in Chapter 5
Barclay Report	Report produced in 1981 to redefine the purpose of social work, emphasising 'community social work'	Summarised in Chapter 4
Beveridge Report	Key report produced in 1942, blueprint for welfare state; actual title was *Social Insurance and Allied Services*	Covered in detail in Chapter 3
Carers	Unpaid people who assist others with special needs, usually relatives but can also be friends or neighbours, essentially volunteers	Term used throughout the book and throughout social work – the term does not apply to social care professionals
Children Act 1948	Principal Act introducing welfare state into children's services, created children's departments and local authorities	Mentioned in Chapter 4
Citizenship	Important concept in social policy, usually attributed to Marshall, focusing on what people must have in order to participate fully in society	Concept explored in more detail in Chapter 3, also in Chapter 7
Classic liberalism	Political perspective or theory connected to classical economic theory, promotes freedom from state intervention and operation of free market forces	Usually referred to as liberalism in this book, explained in more detail in Chapter 3
Classical economic theory	Theory that suggests that market regulation is unnecessary since people will naturally pursue their own interests by buying or selling goods or engaging in the labour market	Theory explained in more detail in Chapter 2
Commodification	Converting a service into a 'product' which is bought and sold on the open market, opposed by proponents of welfare state who argue for decommodification	Relevant to Chapter 7 and discussion of Esping-Anderson typology

Community care	Care in the community in its broadest sense, not just in people's own homes, but also in residential care, in effect any kind of care outside hospital	General term used in social policy and social work, but note includes residential care
Critical thinking	Ability to analyse, evaluate and assess, and to draw conclusions on the basis of weighing up arguments	All of this book has hopefully developed your critical thinking skills
Decommodification	Preventing services being bought and sold on the open market by insisting on state control and regulation, especially of welfare services	Explained in more detail in Chapter 7
Deinstitutionalisation	Moving people out of long-stay institutions, such as long-stay hospitals and Poor Law workhouses	An important theme in Chapter 4
Demography, demographic	To do with population, usually in the sense of interpreting statistics and quantitative data	Of particular importance in explaining social policy changes, see Chapters 5–7 especially
Direct payments	Cash payments made by local authorities to service users in order for service users themselves then to purchase the services they need	You will find more explanations in Chapter 6
Edwardian	The period between 1901 and 1910, the reign of King Edward VII	This is the period covered in Chapter 2
Effective demand	In economics the actual demand for goods and services, that is what people are actually prepared to pay here and now	Important part of explanation of economics, see Chapters 2 and 3
Egalitarianism	Belief that people should be more equal, and associated thinking and policy in relation to this	Important principle underpinning social democratic approach
Elders	Term preferred by some people to 'older people', which is the term used in this book	See related discussion in Chapter 5
Empowerment	Giving people power over their own lives, in social policy terms usually through including them in decision-making and policy-making	An important concept throughout social work
Enlightened self-interest	People pursue their own objectives by seeing that it is in their interests to engage in a free market where they negotiate fairly with others	Important term in classical economic theory, see Chapter 2
Equality	A hotly contested concept but generally taken to mean people having the same rights and operating on a level playing field; does not mean people are all the same or are all to be treated in the same way	There is extensive coverage of this in Chapter 4

Fabian	Fabian Society was founded at the end of the nineteenth century; it believes in collective provision instead of the free market, linked to social democratic thinking and influential in promoting the welfare state	Relevant particularly to Chapter 3
Fair Access to Care Services	A system for banding need into distinct categories set out by Department of Health, so only applies in practice to England	Referred to in Chapter 6
Fiscal	Relating to government taxation policy and associated ways of paying for services	Important social policy term
Free-market forces	Operation of the invisible laws of supply and demand whereby markets regulate themselves without legislation since suppliers and customers agree prices themselves	Underpins theories discussed in Chapters 2 and 4
Friedman	Key monetarist thinker	Views summarised in Chapter 4
Green	TH Green is generally credited with first formulating the notion of positive freedom	Explained further in Chapter 3
Griffiths Report	1988 report on community care services, which recommended that local authorities should play the key role in assessing need for services	See Chapter 4
Hayek	Political theorist who argued that equality was incompatible with personal freedom	A summary of his ideas is given in Chapter 4
Ideology	Set of ideas and beliefs that direct objectives and policies, often covert and taken as 'given'	Important sociological concept with great relevance to social policy
Individual budget	An overall budget for a range of services, can include cash or services or a mixture of both	Important aspect of personalisation, see Chapter 6
Individualism, individual responsibility	Emphasis on self and personal responsibility, above all the notion that individuals are responsible to themselves and for their own well-being	Underpinned social policy in Edwardian era covered in Chapter 2, but relevant throughout the book
Ingleby Committee	Produced 1960, report on youth justice in child protection, part of move towards generic social work	Mentioned in Chapter 4
Keynes, Keynesianism	Keynes was a key economic theorist who promoted government intervention in the economy; his ideas were important in explaining background to the development of the welfare state	Covered in some detail in Chapter 3

Liberalism	Political theory or perspective based on belief in freedom from state intervention, closely associated with classical economic theory and belief in free-market forces	Origins explained in Chapter 2, also relevant in explaining social policy developments in Chapter 4
Local Authority Social Services Act 1970	Act which abolished specialist social services and brought the separate strands together under local authority social services departments	Covered in Chapter 4
Marketisation	Process whereby services are organised or reformulated in order to correspond to an economic system based on the principles of the market, including supply, demand, choice and competition.	Particularly relevant to Chapter 4.
Marshall	Key thinker who promoted the notion of citizenship	Mentioned in Chapter 4
Marxism, Marxist	Economic and political theories of Marx contending that human actions and institutions are economically determined and that class struggle is needed to challenge capitalism	Mentioned in Chapter 4
Means test	Investigative process to determine whether or not someone is financially eligible to qualify for state aid	Important mechanism for implementing selectivist policies
Mixed economy	Combination of state, voluntary and private suppliers of goods and services	Often associated with social policy regimes that are neither entirely liberalist nor entirely social democratic, see Chapter 7
Monetarism, monetarist	Economic theory derived from classical economic thinking, implements policies that promote operation of free-market forces	Covered in Chapter 4
Moral panics	Sociological term referring to process whereby major concerns are created and promoted regarding specific issues or particular groups in society	Mentioned in Introduction since some people say concern about the ageing population is an example of a moral panic
Mortality	In a social policy context used to refer to statistics, namely the number of people who die and the death rate	Covered in more detail in Chapter 5
National Assistance Act 1948	Important Act that formally abolished the Poor Law and heralded the introduction of the welfare state	Mentioned in Chapter 3

National Insurance	State-run system of paying benefits to people in certain circumstances, such as sickness or retirement, financed by compulsory levy usually on wages and salaries	First introduced into Britain in the Edwardian period covered in Chapter 2, then extensively developed in the period covered by Chapter 3
National Service Framework For Older People	Government policy statement on expectations of levels and kinds of services offered to older people	Referred to in Chapter 6
Negative freedom	Freedom from state intervention	Important social policy concept
Neo-classical economic theory	Theories such as monetarism that reinterpret original classical economic theory	Covered in Chapter 4
Neo-liberalism	Updated version of liberalism, came to prominence in Britain in the 1980s	Covered in Chapter 4
New Labour	Policies and approaches adopted by the Labour Party post-1997, based on the reformulation of original social democratic Labour Party principles that led to the establishment of the welfare state	Covered in some detail in Chapter 4
New Right	Resurgence of liberalist political ideas together with classical economic theory, came to prominence in the 1980s across Europe, political aspect of neo-liberalism	Covered in Chapter 4
Normalisation	Reintegration into the community of people formerly set apart from mainstream society in institutions	Mentioned in Chapter 4, there is a section on this in Williams (2009)
Nozick	Political thinker, concerned with notions of freedom, believed someone is entitled to have what they have so long as they acquired it legally	His views are summarised in Chapter 4, where there is a comparison with the views of Rawls
Paupers, pauperism	Receiving Poor Law assistance, but also carries assumption of deficiency, therefore a highly pejorative term	Background covered in Chapter 2
Personal budgets	Sometimes used interchangeably with term 'individual budget', but sometimes used as applying only to social care services	For more information see Chapter 6 where there is a section on this
Personalisation	Processes through which service users have rights to services that meet their needs and, crucially, can choose and direct the way in which services are delivered	Covered in considerable detail in Chapter 6

Pluralism	View that power should be shared and groups should participate in decision-making	Important social policy term
Poor Law	Pre-welfare state system whereby assistance centred on the workhouse, was highly stigmatised, based on notions of charity, not entitlement	Important in Chapter 2, and its abolition (covered in Chapter 3) was an important landmark
POPP	Partnership of Older People Projects, primarily person-centred projects integrating health, well-being and independence	Covered in some detail in Chapter 6
Positive freedom	Belief that people are only free in any meaningful sense if they have certain basic needs met and thereby can participate fully in society	Covered in some detail in Chapter 2, but also of particular relevance to Chapter 7
Postcode lottery	Quality of services offered depends on where someone lives, with high-quality services in some areas and poor quality in others	One of the principles of welfare state is to equalise services and thereby avoid this
Postmodernism	Wide-ranging term which in academic disciplines refers to reaction against notions of objective reality. Instead reality is socially constructed and may be relative to individual or culture so is fallible and relative, rather than certain and universal.	Mentioned in Introduction. Has had some influence on social policy as an academic subject.
Poverty	Lack of ability to pay for basic necessities (absolute poverty) or lack of wealth compared with other people (relative poverty)	There is a section on this in Chapter 5
Rawls	Philosopher who believed that some inequality was inevitable but promoted his 'maximin' strategy that everyone should have the opportunity to play on a relatively level playing field	His views are summarised in Chapter 4, where they are compared to Nozick
Redistribution of wealth	Reallocating resources away from the rich to the poor not just through taxation and provision of state financial benefits but also by creation of services used by the poor but paid for by those with wealth	Important social policy concept, underpins social democratic approaches to social policy
Residual, residualism	Policies whereby state intervenes only where individuals are in dire social need	Generally associated with liberalist policies, see Chapter 3
Resource allocation system	System for determining the size of personal or individual budgets through scoring or assessing specific aspects of needs	For further information see Chapter 6

Scientific rationalist approach	System of categorising needs and devising systems for responding, usually through creation of specialist institutions	Explained further in Chapter 2
Seebohm Report	Influential government report published in 1968 which led to the creation of unified, generic local authority social services departments	Mentioned in Chapter 4
Selectivity, selectivist	Opposite of universalist, system whereby services and benefits are available only to those who qualify, principally through means testing	Key aspect of liberalist policies, discussed further in Chapters 3 and 7
Self-directed support	A variety of approaches to creating personalised social care in order to achieve independent living	There is a section on this in Chapter 6
Smith, Adam	Key eighteenth-century economic thinker, generally credited with developing classical economic theory	His theories are explained in Chapter 2
Social democracy, social democratic	Combination of socialism and democracy, meaning belief that capitalism can be transformed democratically to serve the needs of people, particularly through the welfare state	Important in explaining developments in Chapter 3 and also covered extensively in Chapter 7
Social exclusion	Process whereby certain groups are pushed to the margins of society and prevented from full participation	See discussion in Chapter 5
Statutory social services	Services have to be provided by law and are regulated by Parliament	Generally introduced into the UK in period covered by Chapter 3
Tawney	Political thinker who regarded the existence and approval of inequality an affront to human beings.	There is a summary of his views in Chapter 3
Third Way	Associated with New Labour, belief that there is a policy route between non-interventionist liberalism and state-dominated social democracy	Explained further in Chapter 4
Universalism, universalist	A system whereby benefits and services are available to all, so removing the need for a means test	Key aspects of social democratic policies, discussed further in Chapters 3 and 7
Welfare state	System whereby the state takes the major responsibility for providing for people's needs, and in which the state runs the majority of services	Most of Chapter 3 is about this

Workhouse   Institution where people were required to   Explained further in
reside as a condition of accepting basic   Chapter 2
necessities, where they were required to work
to pay for the charity they were receiving

References

ADASS/DoH (2009) *Common Resource Allocation Framework.* London: Association of Directors of Adult Social Services/Department of Health.

ADASS/LGA (2009) *Implementing Personalisation.* London: Association of Directors of Adult Social Services/Local Government Association.

Age Concern (2008) *Later Life as an Older Lesbian, Gay or Bisexual Person.* London: Age Concern.

Alcock, C., Daly, G. and Griggs, E. (2008) *Introducing Social Policy* (2nd edition), Harlow: Pearson Education.

Alcock, P. (2008) *Social Policy in Britain* (3rd edition). Basingstoke: Palgrave.

Alcock, P., Erskine, A. and May, M. (2008) *The Student's Companion to Social Policy* (3rd edition). Oxford: Blackwell.

Alcock, P., May, M. and Rowlingson, K. (eds.) (2008) *The Student's Companion to Social Policy* (3rd edition). Oxford: Blackwell.

Arksey, H. and Glendinning, C. (2008) Combining Work and Care: Carers' Decision-making in the Context of Competing Policy Pressures. *Social Policy and Administration,* 42 (1): 1–18.

Baldock, J., Manning, N. and Vickerstaff, S. (2007) *Social Policy* (3rd edition). Oxford: Oxford University Press.

Banks, S. (2006) *Ethics and Values in Social Work* (3rd edition). Basingstoke: Palgrave.

Banks, J., Breeze, E., Lessof, C. and Nazroo, J. (eds.) (2008) *English Longitudinal Study of Ageing.* London: Institute for Fiscal Studies.

Barber, B., Devaney, and Stroud, P. (2009) *What are the Implications of Attitudes to Economic Inequality?* London: Joseph Rowntree Foundation.

Bartlett, J. (2009) *Getting More for Less.* London: King's Fund.

Bernard (2007) *A New Strategy for Carers: Better Support for Families and Carers of Older People.* London: Counsel and Care.

Biggs, S., Phillipson, C., Money, A-M. and Leach, R. (2006) The Age Shift: Observations on Social Policy, Ageism and the Dynamics of the Adult Lifecourse. *Journal of Social Work Practice,* 20 (3): 239–50.

Bochel, H., Bochel, C., Page, R. and Sykes, R. (eds.) (2009) *Social Policy: Issues and Developments* (2nd edition). London: Pearson.

Bornat, J. and Leece, J. (eds.) (2006) *Developments in Direct Payments.* Bristol: Policy Press.

Brewer, C. and Lait, J. (1980) Can Social Work Survive? *Journal of Social Policy,* 10: 573–75.

Brown, K. (2010) *Vulnerable Adults and Community Care* (2nd edition). Exeter: Learning Matters.

Brown, K. and Rutter, L. (2008) *Critical Thinking for Social Work (2nd* edition). Exeter: Learning Matters.

Care Quality Commission (2010) *The State of Health Care and Social Care in England.* London: HMSO.

Care Quality Commission (2009) *The Quality and Capacity of Adult Social Care Services.* London: HMSO.

Caring Choice (2008) *Who will pay for long-term care? The future of Care Funding.* London: Time for Change. Available at http://www.caringchoices.org.uk

Cass, E., Robbins, D. and Richardson, A. (2009) *Dignity in Care.* London: SCIE.

Chan, C., Cole, B. and Bowpitt, G. (2007) Welfare State Without Dependency: The Case of the UK Chinese People. *Social Policy and Society,* 6 (4): 503–14.

Charles, N., Davies, C. and Harris, C. (2004) *Family Formation and Kin Relationships: 40 Years of Social Change.* www.esrcsocietytoday.ac.uk

Chau, C. and Yu, S. (2010) The Sensitivity of United Kingdom Healthcare Services to the Diverse Needs of Chinese Origin Older People. *Ageing and Society,* 30: 383–401.

Chen, H. (2009) Successful Ageing Amongst Older People Needing Care: International Comparisons Seeking Solutions. *Social and Public Policy Review,* 3 (1): 1–16.

Chou, R. J-A. (2010) Willingness to Live in Eldercare Institutions Among Older Adults in Urban and Rural China: A Nationwide Study. *Ageing and Society,* 30: 583–608.

Christopoulos, M. and Bromage, V. (2009) What Does *'Career' Mean to People in their 60th Year? Reflections, projections and interpretations by people born in the late 1940s.* Derby: International Centre for Guidance Studies and TAEN.

Clarke, J. (1993) *A Crisis in Care? Challenges to Social Work.* London: Sage.

Cloos, P., Allen, C., Alvarado, B., Zunzunegui, M., Simeon, D. and Eldemire-Shearerk, D. (2010) Active Ageing: A Qualitative Study in Six Caribbean Countries. *Ageing and Society,* 30: 79–101.

Concannon, L. (2009) Developing Inclusive Health and Social Care Policies for Older LGBT Citizens. *British Journal of Social Work,* 39 (3): 403–17.

Conway, L. and McLaughlan, B. (2005) *Old People and Eye Tests.* London: RNIB. Available at http://www. rnib.org.uk

Cook, J. (2010) Exploring Older Women's Citizenship: Understanding the Impact of Migration in Later Life. *Ageing and Society,* 30: 253–73.

Cottrell, S. (2008) *The Study Skills Handbook* (3rd edition). Basingstoke: Palgrave.

Craig, R. and Mindell, J. (eds) *(2005) Health Survey for England.* London: NHS Information Centre.

Crawford, K. and Walker, J. (2008) *Social Work with Older People* (2nd edition). Exeter: Learning Matters.

Davis, H. and Ritters, K. (2009) *LinkAge Plus National Evaluation: End of Project Report.* London: Department for Work and Pensions.

Department of Health (2010) *The Future of Social Work in Adult Social Services in England.* London: Department of Health.

Department of Health (2009) *Shaping the Future of Care Together.* London: Department of Health.

Department of Health (2008) *Carers at the Heart of 21st-century Families and Communities.* London: Department of Health.

Department of Health (2006) *Our Health, Our Care, Our Say.* London: Department of Health.

Department of Health (2005a) *Building Telecare in England.* London: Department of Health.

Department of Health (2005b) *Independence, Well-being and Choice.* London: Department of Health.

Department of Health (2002) *Fair Access to Care Services.* London: Department of Health.

Department of Health (2001) *National Service Framework for Older People.* London: Department of Health.

Social Work, Social Policy and Older People

Department of Health (2000) *A Quality Strategy for Social Care.* London: Department of Health.

Department of Health (1999) *National Strategy for Carers.* London: Department of Health.

Department of Health (1998) *Modernising Social Services.* London: Department of Health.

Department of Work and Pensions (2006) *A Sure Start to Later Life.* London: Office of the Deputy Prime Minister.

Dickens, J. (2010) Social *Work and Social Policy: An Introduction.* Abingdon: Routledge.

Digby, A. (1989) *British Welfare Policy: Workhouse To Workfare.* London: Faber and Faber.

Drake, R. (2001) *The Principles of Social Policy.* Basingstoke: Paigrave.

Ellis (2007) Direct Payments and Social Work Practice: The Significance of 'Street-Level Bureaucracy' in Determining Eligibility. *British Journal of Social Work,* 37 (3): 405–22.

Esping-Anderson, G. (1990) *The Three Worlds of Welfare Capitalism.* Oxford: Polity Press.

Esping-Anderson, G. (1996) *Welfare States in Transition.* London: Sage.

Finch, J. and Mason, J. (1993) *Negotiating Family Responsibilities.* London: Tavistock/Routledge.

Ford, J. and Sinclair, R. (1987) *Sixty Years On: Women Talk About Old Age.* London: Women's Press.

Gladstone, D. (1999) *The Twentieth Century Welfare State.* Basingstoke: Palgrave.

Glasby, J. (2009) Adult Health and Social Care, in Bochel, H., Bochel, C., Page, R. and Sykes, R. (eds) *Social Policy: Themes Issues and Debates* (2nd edition). Harlow: Pearson.

Glendinning, C., Arksey, H., Tjadens, F., Moree, M., Moran, N. and Nies, H. (2009) Care Provision Within Families and its Socio-economic Impact on Care Providers Across the European Union. *Research Works, 2009–05.* York: Social Policy Research Unit, University of York.

Glendinning, C., Challis, D., Fernandez, J., Jacobs, S., Jones, K., Knapp, M., Manthorpe, J., Moran, N., Netten, A., Stevens, M. and Wilberforce, M. (2008) *Evaluation of the Individual Budgets Pilot Programme: Final Report.* York: Social Policy Research Unit, University of York.

Griffin, J. and Tyrrell, I. (2003) *Human Givens: A New Approach to Emotional Health and Clear Thinking.* Chalvington: HG Publishing.

Griffiths, R. (1988) *Community Care: Agenda for Action.* London: HMSO.

Gustafsson, B., Johansson, M. and Palmer, E. (2009) The Welfare of Sweden's Old-age Pensioners in Times of Bust and Boom from 1990. *Ageing and Society,* 29: 539–61.

Haberkern, K. and Szydlik, M. (2010) State Care Provision, Societal Opinion and Children's Care of Older Parents in 11 European Countries. *Ageing and Society,* 30: 299–323.

Harris, J. (2008) State Social Work: Constructing the Present from Moments in the Past. *British Journal of Social Work,* 38: 662–79.

Harrop, A., Jopling, K. and contributors (2009) *One Voice: Shaping Our Ageing Society.* London: Age Concern and Help the Aged.

Hennessy, P. (1992) *Never Again.* London: Penguin.

Hicks, J. and Allen, G. (1999) *A Century of Change: Trends in UK Statistics Since 1900.* London: House of Commons.

Hill, M. (2003) *Understanding Social Policy* (7th edition). Oxford: Blackwell.

Hill, M. and Irving, Z. (2009) *Understanding Social Policy* (8th edition). Oxford: Wiley-Blackwell.

Hirsch, D. (2005) *Facing the Cost of Long-term Care: Towards a Sustainable Funding System.* York: Joseph Rowntree Foundation.

HM Government (2010) *Building a Safe and Confident Future: Implementing the Recommendations of the Social Work Task Force.* London: Department for Children, Schools and Families.

HM Government (2008) *Carers at the Heart of 21st Century Families.* London: Department of Health.

HM Government (2007) *Putting People First: A Shared Vision and Commitment to the Transformation of Adult Social Care*. London: Department of Health.

Holloway, M. (2009) Dying Old in the 21st century: A Neglected Issue for Social Work.*International Social Work*, 52 (6): 713–25.

Holloway, M. and Lymbery, M. (2007) Editorial – Caring for People: Social Work with Adults in the Next Decade and Beyond. *British Journal of Social Work*, 37: 375–86.

Humphries, R., Forder, J. and Fernández, J-L. (2010) *Securing Good Care for More People: Options for Reform*. London: King's Fund.

Ice, G., Yogo, J., Heh, V. and Juma, E. (2010) The Impact of Caregiving on the Health and Well-being of Kenyan Luo Grandparents. *Research on Aging*, 32 (1.): 40–66. London: Sage.

IFSW (2000) Definition of Social Work. International Federation of Social Workers. Available at www.ifsw.org

Jeon, H-S. and Dunkle, R. (2009) Stress and Depression Among the Oldest-Old: A Longitudinal Analysis. *Research on Ageing*, 31: 661–87. London: Sage.

Johansson, L., Sundström, G. and Hassing, L. (2003) State Provision Down, Offspring's Up: The Reverse Substitution of Old-Age Care in Sweden. *Ageing and Society*, 23: 269–80.

Jones, S. (2009) *Critical Learning for Social Work Students*. Exeter: Learning Matters.

King's Fund (2008) *The Future of Care Funding: Time for a change*. London: King's Fund.

Kwon, H., Mkandawire, T. and Palme, J. (2009) Introduction: Social Policy and Economic Development in Late industrializers. *International Journal of Social Welfare*, 18 (S1): S1–S11.

Langley, J. (2001) Developing Anti-oppressive Empowering Social Work Practice with Older Lesbian Women and Gay Men. *British Journal of Social Work*, 24 (1/2): 29–42.

Lavalette, M. and Pratt, A. (2005) *Social Policy: Theories, Concepts and Issues*. London: Sage.

Lawrence, S. and Simpson G. (2009) International Aspects of Social Work with Elders, in Lawrence, S. et al. (eds.) *Introducing International Social Work*. Exeter: Learning Matters.

Lawrence, S., Lyons, K., Simpson, G. and Huegler, N. (eds.) (2009) *Introducing International Social Work*. Exeter: Learning Matters.

Leadbetter, C. (2004) *Personalisation Through Participation*. London: Demos.

Leadbetter, C., Bartlett, J. and Gallagher, N. (2008) *Making it Personal*, London: Demos.

Lishman, G. (2006) *The Whole of Me . . . Meeting the Needs of Old Lesbians, Gay Men and Bisexuals Living in Care Homes and Extra Care Housing: A resource Pack for Professionals*. London: SCIE. Available at http: //www.scie-socialcareonline.org.uk

Lloyd, J. (2009) *Caring in the Older Population*. London: ILC.

Lymbery, M. (2010) A New Vision for Adult Social Care? Continuities and Change in the Care of Older People. *Critical Social Policy*, 30 (1): 5–26.

Lymbery, M. (2005) *Social Work with Older People*. London: Sage.

McIntosh, K. (2008) *Under the Radar: BME Mental Health*. www.hsj.co.uk/lunder-the-radar-bme-mental-health/1731708.article

Manthorpe, J. and others (2009) Training for Change: Early Days of Individual Budgets and the Implications for Social Work and Care Management: A Qualitative Study of the Views of Trainers. *British Journal of Social Work*, 39: 1291–1305.

Manthorpe, J. and Stevens, M. (2009) Increasing Care Options in the Countryside: Developing an Understanding of the Potential Impact of Personalization for Social Work with Rural Older People. *British Journal of Social Work*. Advance Access published online on 27 March, 10. 1093/bjsw/bcp038

Manthorpe, J., Stevens, M., Rapaport, J., Harris, J., Jacobs, S., Challis, D., Netten, A., Knapp, M., Wilberforce, M. and Glendinning, C. (2009) Safeguarding and System Change: Early Perceptions of the Implications for Adult Protection Services of the English Individual Budgets Pilots: A Qualitative Study. *British Journal of Social Work*, 39, 1465–80.

Marmot, M. (2010) *Fair Society, Healthy Lives: The Marmot Review*. London: Department of Health.

Means, R. (1995) Older People and the Personal Social Services, in Gladstone, D. (ed) *British Social Welfare: Past, Present and Future*. London: UCL Press.

Midwinter, E. (1994) *The Development of Social Welfare in Britain*. Buckingham: Open University Press.

Millar, J. (2003) Social Policy and Family Policy, in Alcock P., Erskine A. and May M. (eds.) *The Student's Companion to Social Policy*. Oxford: Blackwell.

Mind (2005) *Mind Exposes Severe Neglect of Older People*. www.mind.org.uk/news/2069_mind_exposes_severe_neglect_of_older_people

Mold, F., Fitzpatrick, J. and Roberts, J. (2005) Caring for Minority Ethnic Older People in Nursing Care Homes. *British Journal of Nursing*, 14 (11): 601–606.

Moriarty, I. and Butt, J. (2004) Inequalities in Quality of Life Among Older People from Different Ethnic Groups. *Ageing and Society*, 24: 729–53.

Munthree, C. (2010) Growing Old in the Era of a High Prevalence of HIV/AIDS: The Impact of AIDS on Older Men and Women in KwaZulu-Natal, South Africa. *Research on Ageing*, 32 (2), 155–74.

Musingarimi, P. (2008) *Health Issues Affecting Older Gay, Lesbian and Bisexual People in the UK. A Policy Brief.* **www.ilcuk.org.uk**

Netto, G. (1998) 'I forget myself': The case for provision of culturally sensitive respite services of minority ethnic carers of old people. *Journal of Public Health Medicine*, 29 (2): 221–26. Available at www. jpubhealth.oxfordjournals.org

O'Brien, M. and Penna, S. (1998) *Theorising Welfare*. London: Sage.

OECD (2010) *Health at a Glance 2009: Key Findings for the United States*. Available at **www.oecd.org**

Payne, M. (2005) *The Origins of Social Work: Continuity and Change*. Basingstoke: Palgrave.

Powell, F. (2001) *The Politics of Social Work*. London: Sage.

Price, E. (2008) Pride or Prejudice? Gay Men, Lesbians and Dementia. *British Journal of Social Work*, 38 (3): 1337–52.

QAA (2008) *Subject Benchmarks for Social Work*. York: QAA. Available at **www.qaa.ac.uk**

QAA (2007) *Subject Benchmarks for Social Policy*. York: QAA. Available at **www.qaa.ac.uk**

Ray, M., Bernard, M. and Phillips, J. (2009) *Critical Issues in Social Work with Older People*. Basingstoke: Palgrave.

Reisman, D. (2009) *Social Policy in an Ageing Society: Age and Health in Singapore*. Cheltenham: Edward Elgar Publishing.

RNID (2005) *About deafness and hearing loss: Statistics*. London: RNID. Available at http://www.rnid.org.uk

SCIE (2010) *Personalisation: A Rough Guide* (revised edition). London: Social Care Institute for Excellence.

Scottish Executive (2006) *Changing Lives: Report of the 21st Century Social Work Review*. Edinburgh: Scottish Executive.

Scourfield, P. (2007) Social Care and the Modern Citizen: Client, Consumer, Service User, Manager and Entrepreneur. *British Journal of Social Work*, 37: 107–22.

Seebohm Report (1968) Report of the Committee on Local Authority and Allied Personal Social Services, Cmnd 3703. London: HMSO.

Sharkey, P. (2007) *The Essentials of Community Care* (2nd edition). Basingstoke: Palgrave.

Sundström, G., Malmberg, B. and Johansson, L. (2006) Balancing Family and State Care: Neither, Either or Both? The Case of Sweden. *Ageing and Society*, 26: 767–82.

Sutherland, S. (1999) *With Respect to Old Age: Long-Term Care – Rights and Responsibilities: A Report by the Royal Commission on Long-Term Care*. London: HMSO.

Theurer, K. and Wister, A. (2010) Altruistic Behaviour and Social Capital as Predictors of Well-being Among Older Canadians. *Ageing and Society*, 30: 157–81.

Thompson, P. (1992) *The Edwardians*. London: Routledge.

Townsend, P. (1979) *Poverty in the United Kingdom: A Survey of Households and Standards of Living*. Berkeley: University of California Press.

UN (2009) *World Population Ageing*. New York: United Nations Department of Economic and Social Affairs Population Division.

Walker, A. and Walker, C. (1998) Normalisation and 'Normal' Ageing: The Social Construction of Dependency Among Older People with Learning Difficulties. *Disability and Society*, 13 (1): 125–42.

Walker, H. (2008) *Studying for Your Social Work Degree*. Exeter: Learning Matters.

Williams, F. (1989) *Social Policy: A Critical Introduction*. Cambridge: Polity Press.

Williams, P. (2009) *Social Work with People with Learning Difficulties* (2nd edition). Exeter: Learning Matters.

Windle, K., Wagland, R., Forder, J., D'Amico, F., Janssen, D. and Wistow, G. (2010) *National Evaluation of Partnerships for Older People Projects*. London: Department of Health.

Zahno, K. and Rhule, C. (2008) *Information and Advice Needs of Black and Minority Ethnic Older People In England. Report to Age Concern England*. London: Age Concern.

Index

Added to the page reference 'g' denotes the glossary and 't' denotes a table.